W9-BJC-260

LIKE A RIVER

Finding the Faith and Strength to Move Forward After Loss and Heartache

GRANGER SMITH

W Publishing Group
An Imprint of Thomas Nelson

Like a River

Published in Nashville, Tennessee, by W Publishing, an imprint of Thomas Nelson.

The author is represented by The Fedd Agency.

Thomas Nelson titles may be purchased in bulk for educational, business, fundraising, or sales promotional use. For information, please email SpecialMarkets@ThomasNelson.com.

ISBN 978-1-4003-3439-1 (audiobook)
ISBN 978-1-4003-3438-4 (eBook)
ISBN 978-1-4003-3436-0 (HC)
ISBN 978-1-4003-4027-9 (signed)

Library of Congress Control Number: 2022950300

Printed in the United States of America

23 24 25 26 27 LBC 5 4 3 2 1

To my wife, Amber—
There's no one else on earth I'd rather ride this wild river with than you. You take me by the hand and love me for the man I almost am.

CONTENTS

1

THE WATER'S EDGE

He sent from on high, he took me; he
drew me out of many waters.

2 Samuel 22:17

SOAK IN THIS MOMENT BECAUSE *it won't last forever.*

It was the last thought I remember having before everything changed.

Texas summers are not for the faint of heart, but in early spring and into the first few weeks of June, the weather is tough to beat. I was barefoot, enjoying a beautiful, relaxing evening out in the backyard spotting my daughter, London, as she did a handstand. London was seven at the time. The oldest of our three kids, the planner in the group, and the one who thinks through every step she takes, London is hyperaware of everyone's emotions. So much so that she intuitively knows how you are feeling and is ready to be there for you. She's a treasure to all who are around her. On this particular Tuesday evening she was excited to show me the new gymnastics routine she had just created.

Meanwhile our boys, Lincoln and River, were in another part of the yard having a water gun fight. Lincoln, who was five years old at the time, is an entertainer at heart. He is the one who will do anything to get a laugh from whatever audience he can gather. And if there is a competition involved, he's going to be right there in the middle of it. He was also always quick to invite River, his best friend in the entire world, along for the ride. Lincoln, a tough but sensitive kid who unashamedly wears his love on his sleeve for everyone to see, never worries or complains.

At the time our youngest, River, was a three-year-old, outgoing extrovert who was always on the move. He spent most of his time spinning plastic tires on his battery-powered riding tractor or squatting on his heels, dragging a toy excavator across the dirt. In whatever he was doing, River kept a hand free to clutch his scuffed-up Lightning McQueen Hot Wheels car between his sweet but most often dirty little fingers.

It was about as wonderful an evening as any dad could ask for, and I wanted to soak up every second. Even more so because my bags were already packed for the trip I was taking the next day. The first stop was Nashville, Tennessee, for the CMT Music Awards.

My career in country music was flying high. We were touring with the top artists, playing stadiums, arenas, and some of the nation's largest amphitheaters. Our own headlining tickets and tours were in high demand, and every song I put out seemed to work. We were getting a ton of airplay on the radio, topping Billboard charts, and getting invitations to all the industry music award shows.

The invitations are always an honor to receive, but these ceremonies are far from my favorite way to spend an evening. To be honest, I don't like them at all. They are hot, stuffy, and time-consuming. Plus, I've never really enjoyed dressing up. (By the way, the bright lights on those red carpets make every piece of lint stand out.)

The red-carpet experience itself is a long, drawn-out waiting game in the media gauntlet. Each talent, with their respective publicist, mingles down the aisle for hours, weaving through the journalists who represent the smaller media outlets while waiting for a turn with the more influential mainstream ones. The actual show is a relief because after a couple of hours of shaking hands and taking pictures, you're finally able to sit down. Then, after all the awards are dished out, it's several hours of record label and agent parties because behind any successful music career is a ton of people who have worked unbelievably hard. It's why I always do my best to attend and show my gratitude.

But it makes for a long night.

We were set to head out on tour the day after the awards

ceremony. Summer is a fun time to be on the road because it means music festivals and fairs. It also means I can usually bring my family with me. The kids are out of school and love riding in my tour bus, Wildflower, waking up each morning in a new town, at a new fairground, with a new Ferris wheel, and the promise of even more cotton candy.

Topping charts, winning awards, touring with my friends and family—life was good. Better than good. Being a country music singer was everything I'd dreamed of since my dad took me to see George Strait at the Alamodome in San Antonio. I was sixteen at the time and excited for the experience, but I had no idea just how life-altering it would be.

The show blew me away.

Every last piece of it.

As we drove home I knew I had to be a part of that crazy circus. And if I wasn't the star, that was okay too. I didn't care if I was the lighting guy, the bus driver, or the security crew; whatever it took, I wanted to live that lifestyle. Yet, on this particular Tuesday evening in early June, as I stood in the backyard with my kids, I realized all I ever *really* wanted was to be present in this moment—at home with my incredible family.

Soak in this moment because it won't last forever.

SOAK IN THIS MOMENT BECAUSE IT WON'T LAST FOREVER.

I didn't realize, as I helped my daughter with her handstand, just how true those words were, because they were immediately interrupted by another thought: *The boys are quiet. Where's River?*

EVERY PARENT'S WORST NIGHTMARE

"Where's River?" was a standard question in our house. His constant movement fed his drive to be an explorer on the search for the next adventure. It was commonplace for me to have to take off out of our house and run into the woods in an effort to catch our barefoot son who had bolted out, still dressed in his pajamas.

The boy was wild. Like a river.

That's when I found him.

I glanced over my left shoulder, and my heart stopped. I saw every parent's worst nightmare. Just fifteen paces away from me, inside our gated and locked pool, I saw River in the water, facedown.

His normally active little body wasn't moving.

Fear gripped me.

London shrieked, and I took off running as the whole world began to spin around me. I rushed to the pool, flung the gate open, crashed into the water, and picked him up. Expecting him to cough and spit, I was already rehearsing my speech: "Riv! How'd you get in here? You scared me, buddy!"

But I never got to say those words to him.

He was lifeless and cold—like a doll. His face and arms were purple, and his brown eyes were wide open, rolling around aimlessly in his head.

Panic devoured me.

How many minutes since I'd last seen him? One? Maybe two? How could he be unconscious like this?

I didn't know. I had no answers. All I knew to do was start

CPR as I shouted at London to run to the house and get Amber, my wife, who was inside taking a shower. Fortunately, Amber had heard London scream, so she had already burst into action and was running outside to the pool.

I'll never forget her face in that moment—sheer terror masked in disbelief. She looked at me and then down to our lifeless boy cradled in my arms.

I broke her shock with my words, "Go get your phone! Call 911!"

Meanwhile, I was alone, with River lying unresponsive in my arms.

Okay, how do I do this? I'd seen CPR performed in movies before, but that was it.

Compress the chest and count one, two, three, four?

Breathe into his mouth?

Amber returned, eyes full of fear. "Wake up, baby, wake up," she kept repeating. "Come on, wake up, Riv! Please, Jesus. Oh *please*, God, no!"

The 911 dispatcher deliberately and calmly walked us through what to do and what to expect when the EMTs arrived. Every second felt like a lifetime.

Amber and I traded off CPR attempts until we finally heard the sirens coming from across the farmland. There were lots of them; it sounded like an entire army. But sound travels far in the country, so I knew they were still miles away.

"Come on, River. Wake up," I kept saying. A prayer that was more of a plea. Occasionally the pressure in his body from the CPR attempts would force water out of his mouth. It almost sounded like a cough . . . but it wasn't. We would think we were making progress only to be let down once again. Still, we kept at it.

A LOSS TOO DEEP FOR WORDS

The sirens grew louder and louder as they came screaming down our typically quiet country road. To keep from losing precious time, London wisely ran out in front of the house to wave them down and direct them to the backyard. Remember, she was only seven at the time. It didn't sink in until much later just how hard that must have been for her to endure, especially after seeing her brother in that way. Not to mention the tremendous bravery she showed, rallying with wisdom beyond her age in the face of unimaginable tragedy.

Upon arrival, the EMTs immediately started their lifesaving procedures. They were able to get his heart beating again, but the problem was his brain. The ten minutes it took for the ambulance to drive to our country home had cost him severely; that was a *long* time for his brain to go without oxygen.

Amber shielded the older kids from the view of the scene, while police officers meticulously asked me about the accident. My heart raced as I listened and answered their monotonous, routine questions. When the emergency responders strapped River onto a gurney to rush him to the hospital, I loaded the family into our car to follow. I looked back at the many officers walking around the house and hollered, "Are you all staying here?" One coldly responded, "Yes. This is a crime scene." Another, feeling empathy in the situation, said, "Go. Follow your little boy. We'll lock up the house when we finish here."

In the PICU, River was surrounded by a team of doctors who were doing everything they could to save him. We stayed with him in his room, sitting, crying, and praying to God for a miracle.

But the miracle didn't come.

As night fell, London and Lincoln went home with close friends of our family, but Amber and I stayed in the room with Riv while other family members and friends camped in the waiting room. Sometime during the night, amid the beeping heart monitor and periodic doctor interruptions, I noticed in my delirium that I was still wearing damp blue jeans and boots with no socks. I slid off the old boots over blisters that had formed on my toes. In such a hurry to leave, I must have forgotten to put on socks, but it didn't matter at this point. If I had a thousand blisters, I still wouldn't have felt them over the pain in my heart.

The next day a team of neurologists met with us to deliver the worst news a parent could ever hear—they were unable to find any brain activity, which means there was zero chance that River would recover. We had zero chance of seeing our perfect baby boy on this earth ever again.

IT'S A LOSS, A PAIN, AN ACHE THAT IS TOO DEEP FOR WORDS.

Absolutely nothing can prepare you for that moment. The moment you have to say goodbye to your child. The moment you must leave the hospital with one less person than you arrived with.

It's a loss, a pain, an ache that is too deep for words.

WHAT PAIN IS NOT

When grief is really bad, it's a reflection of a love that was really great. The deeper you love someone, the more you'll grieve their loss. That's why certain losses—death, separation, divorce, and breakups of any kind that involve the heart and emotions—affect us more than other losses do.

The truth is, I had no idea how to deal with this kind of pain.

It broke into my world like a thief and stole my joy, my passion for life, my sanity, and it replaced them with something far more sinister: guilt. My journey forward was messy, vulnerable, and agonizing.

It just about killed me.

It's why I wanted to write this book. My hope is that sharing the details of our story will help you with the challenging details of yours.

Maybe you've experienced a deep loss or you're currently suffering from grief or guilt. Maybe you're reading this book because, like me, you've had to bury someone who meant the world to you. Or maybe you've watched the person you desperately love walk out of your life forever. Maybe you've felt that terrible, heart-stopping, gut-wrenching experience of watching your world be pulled away from you, and you know there is nothing you can do about it.

Even if none of these fit exactly where you are right now, I need you to know that loss is a natural part of life. In fact, it's not a matter of *if*; it's a matter of *when*. And although it's always painful, I've learned two important truths:

1. Pain is not permanent.
2. Pain is not pointless.

You may not currently believe these two truths, which is okay. My hope is that, by the end of this book, you will not just know and believe them in your mind but will also experience the freedom that is available on the other side of the pain. The pain of grief.

Though you can never truly move on from your loss, you *can* move forward. I certainly can't speak for everyone, but I can tell you how it happened for me. And for the record, it was quite a journey to get there.

WELCOME HOME, RIVER

Our drive home from the hospital was long, slow, and mostly silent. Amber and I knew that our kids would be there waiting for us, so we spent most of the time trying to figure out how we would explain what had just happened. Honestly, how do we tell a seven-year-old and five-year-old that their brother wasn't coming home? Ever. London and Lincoln were expecting three of us to show up. In their minds, their little brother was still alive, and every mile we traveled was another minute they were given to believe it was so.

The hospital had a grief counseling team that spoke with us often during our less than sixty hours in the PICU. One thing they were adamant about was that we tell our two living children that River had died. Not to attempt to soften it with words like he was *sleeping*, *resting*, *in a better place*, or any other analogy that pandered to their emotions or possibly led them to the conclusion that they wanted to go there and be with him.

As expected, London and Lincoln were waiting for us in the driveway when we pulled in. The sky was bright blue and painted with high, radiant clouds. The kids had spent the better half of the morning decorating and writing with chalk on the concrete the words they still believed were true: *Welcome home, River!* The mental snapshot I have of them standing beside their message will forever be seared in my memory.

Amber and I rolled up to the house, wishing and wanting to wake up from the nightmare, but we never woke up. This wasn't a nightmare; it was reality. We had to tell the kids the devastating news.

"Where's River?" Lincoln asked as we opened the car door. "Where is he, Momma?"

London knew by our faces. She's very perceptive. She gasped

and put her hands on her mouth. Her words were slow and sad, "Where is he, Daddy?"

I took a deep breath and spoke slowly, "Come here, guys. Let's talk." Amber and I walked them over to an iron bench in the yard. When we were situated, I got right to it. I didn't want to delay it any longer. "River died. His brain didn't have enough oxygen for too long, which made him very sick. Too sick for him to recover."

London immediately began to sob—feeling and voicing all of our pain.

Lincoln stared blankly into the trees behind our house. His five-year-old mind couldn't possibly process that quickly what it meant to return alone to the bedroom that he and his best bud had shared together, and that it would forever be that way.

The four of us sat on that bench and cried, talked, and held one another close. Amber and I answered as many questions as they threw at us. We told them that any emotion they felt at that time was okay. When we had no more tears to cry or questions to answer, we walked hand in hand back to the house, past the pool; and for the first time in three years, our family was again a family of four.

THE DARK PIT

A couple of years before we lost River, I read a book about the importance of establishing a productive morning routine. The author outlined a series of steps that helped me hone the perfect morning to launch me into the rest of my day.

Inspired, I began to set my alarm clock a little earlier, wake up with a purpose, and implement all the principles I found in the book. It was great. I started getting in better shape, felt focused, and had more energy throughout the day. That book is one of thousands on the market categorized as self-help. Millions of them are sold every year, and for good reason. If you've ever read a good one, you know how beneficial they can be. They can help you dream bigger for your life, set attainable goals, stay on track, and accomplish the things you want to achieve.

Self-help really does help—until it doesn't.

When your entire life is falling apart, these books—full of witty one-liners, inspirational quotes, and helpful principles for increasing productivity and achieving your goals—don't help much.

When we lost River, I dug as deep as I could into my self-help toolbox. I tried everything at my fingertips to pull myself out of the dark pit I was in and to relieve the pain I felt.

Nothing helped.

The pit was too dark and too deep to climb out of on my own, and all the self-help, self-improvement, and self-reflection didn't offer relief. The storm was too powerful. The darkness was too dark. I had nothing left.

What I didn't know at the time is that the problem with self-help is in the name. I was trying to help myself out of a place I couldn't escape on my own. I was relying on myself to make the journey into the light, but I didn't have anything left to give.

I couldn't help myself.

I couldn't save myself.

And the more I tried, the darker things got.

THE EXCAVATOR

A week later, on June 11, 2019, we did the unthinkable; we buried our precious little redheaded boy in his blue jeans and bare feet, giving him the last earthly gift we could give him, a custom Lightning McQueen coffin.

The hot summer sun seemed to stand still in the sky as we cried, reflected, and remembered the amazing gift that River's three years on this earth had been for all of us. As we stood at his grave, one tiny cloud crept overhead and brought something very rare for central Texas in June—rain.

Not a lot.

But enough.

Because as we all turned to walk away from the grave, there was a rainbow above us for everyone to see.

Amber, the kids, and our extended family piled into the Sprinter van, and once everyone found a seat, I joined them and closed the sliding door. As I did, I looked back one more time and saw the men pile the remaining scoops of dirt on the mound with their small excavator—River's favorite kind of tractor. I remembered the many times Riv would call to me from his car seat asking me to pull over to the side of the road so we could watch an excavator at work. He loved that machine.

The image hit too close to home. The sick, twisted correlation was too much to handle. My sweet three-year-old boy being buried in the ground by the very tractor that brought him so much life. As we pulled away, leaving our beloved boy in the dirt, I tried to get the image out of my mind, but I couldn't.

Every time I closed my eyes, I saw it. I saw River lying facedown in our pool under my supervision. I saw his lifeless face as I turned him over. I saw the EMTs surrounding him in our backyard, doing everything they could to bring him back as I stood by helplessly with my wife and kids. I saw his breathless body being buried in the earth.

Those images played through my mind on repeat.

Every time I shut my eyes, it felt like I was transported to a cold and empty movie theater that I didn't want to be in but wasn't allowed to leave. I was forced to sit in my seat and watch as the traumatic images repeated on the screen.

It was a never-ending horror show.

I knew it was all in my head, but it felt just as real as anything I had ever experienced.

In addition, Amber and I started receiving criticism and shaming from people online who were blaming us for the incident. I couldn't close my eyes without replaying the horrible nightmare, and I couldn't open my computer without being bombarded by comments and critiques. It was all too much, and I was quickly losing the strength to keep going.

It drove me to a darker place than I'd ever known was possible.

I was broken. Deeply broken. I had known what it was like to have a bad day or even an off week, but this was different. I was broken at the deepest part of me. And all I knew was I needed help.

LIKE A RIVER

Have you ever stood on the bank of a river and watched it run? If you have, you probably noticed that it never stops moving forward—it never stops flowing downstream.

Rivers have a job to do. It's an important job. In fact, since the beginning, humans have been relying on them to keep running. Rivers were the highway system before there were highways, used for trading and transportation. They drain rainwater and provide a habitat for all sorts of living creatures. And if you've ever had to endure an afternoon without running water, you know just how dependent we are on having a source of it nearby. There is a reason so many major cities were built next to a river—rivers help us survive.

But a river's journey isn't always easy. Rivers are full of twists and turns. They get dammed up by barriers, blocked up by debris, and polluted by people. Yet they keep moving forward.

When I stand on the bank of a river and watch it find a way to continue moving forward, I can't help but think rivers have important lessons to teach us.

Like a river, life is full of twists and turns.

Like a river, we will encounter storms, debris, shallows, deep, calm, and turbulence.

But like a river, regardless of the obstacles, there is always a path downstream.

The question is how. What's a river's secret? How does it keep moving forward through so much adversity?

That's what this book is about.

When we lost our son, I thought the pain would never end. Some nights were so long and so dark that I began to wonder if the sun would ever rise—if a new day would ever come.

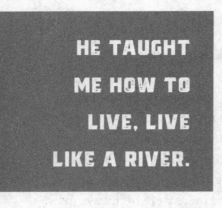

HE TAUGHT ME HOW TO LIVE, LIVE LIKE A RIVER.

I didn't want to talk.

I didn't want to think.

And I certainly didn't want to get back up onstage and sing.

But that wasn't the end of my story. I'm in a different and much better place today.

Getting here hasn't been easy, and it hasn't been quick. Learning to live after loss is not a simple or straightforward process, but I'm here to help you discover that it is possible.

This is a book about that process. It's about learning to live after loss, which actually comes to all of us at some point in life—one way or another. It's also about my journey toward purpose on the other side of debilitating pain.

Ultimately, it's a book about the amazing lesson my son, River, showed me. I may have had only three years to spend with him on this side of eternity, but I'll never forget what I learned—he taught me how to live, live like a river.

2

OUR FOREVER HOME

All streams run to the sea, but the sea is not full;
to the place where the streams
flow, there they flow again.
Ecclesiastes 1:7

THINGS WERE GOOD. REALLY GOOD. You would've said that if you saw it. At the end of a sleepy Texas Hill Country farm road was an iron gate swinging into barbed wire cattle fencing along green bluestem pastures, desert wildflowers, and blooming prickly pear cactuses. Honeybees, butterflies, and hummingbirds frequented the peach and pear trees that framed a crawling gravel road down to the house. This was ten acres of heaven.

For five years I found relief from the hectic life of touring by clearing cedar trees and underbrush and planting a variety of native saplings like pecan, live oak, red oak, cedar, elm, magnolia, and Monterrey oak, just to name a few. I shredded the open pastures and planted new grasses of all varieties. It was home to whitetail deer—a little green oasis where pregnant does would drop their fawns in May. We had cottontails, raccoons, possums, gray squirrels, red foxes, ringtail cats, and just about every variety of wild bird that central Texas has to offer.

When we bought the acreage in 2014, it was rocky, overgrazed, and overgrown by invasive, water-craving cedar trees. I loved the challenge. In just a few years, with the advice of many old farmers, I had created my own little utopia.

The house, positioned toward the front of the property, was a classic Texas ranch design. It had big, shady porches; local limestone; and rustic cedar beams. The views were so beautiful from every window that I even pulled down the white picket fence in the backyard to keep the view uninterrupted from all lines of sight.

It was home.

Amber and I frequently called it our "Forever Home." The

kids could run barefoot and play for hours under the massive live oak canopies. *Am I dreaming?* I had that thought a lot. *What an ideal place to raise three kids!* It's so hard for me to say that sentence out loud now, but that's truly what I thought.

Amber and I were so happy—with our ideal little farmhouse, three kids, two dogs, and a cat—that we decided to take destiny into our own hands by electing to have Amber's fallopian tubes tied, preventing any future pregnancy. With our oars in the water and our boat upright, our river was calm and steady, and we were navigating it smoothly.

Forever home.

Forever family.

Forever bliss.

Forever mistaken.

THE LANDING PAD

After our lives were forever changed, the land was a burden, an unrewarding hardship. The house was dark and lifeless. River's bed was cold and quiet. His toys were stacked neatly in boxes, and his pajamas were folded and in the closet. There was no more of his laughter echoing the halls or dirty bare feet bouncing on the hardwood floors. There were no more squeals of the battery-powered tractor or popcorn kernels in the couch cushions.

Our family pastor walked the property with me before the funeral to get an idea of River's short life and collect imagery for his message. In the backyard he paused at the swimming pool. He stood in silence as his eyes brimmed with tears under his spectacles, and he stared over the pool fence into the blue water. He forced the whispered words over the lump in his throat, "Oh, Granger. Y'all are going to have to move far away from here."

I knew he was right. I couldn't look at that pool every day. It was a murdering thief, masked in tranquil blue, a chlorine-stained death. Our forever home was now only a memory of tragedy.

Sure, we had traveled some rough stretches of water before, but now our river was raging. I did the only thing I had ever done—I dug in deeper with my oars, tried to keep the boat balanced, and steered around the boulders as they came. The first was a big one that I knew would take us out if I didn't act fast.

My family needed a landing pad.

My brother Tyler was selling his home four miles from ours. Only a few weeks after losing Riv, we agreed that I would buy it as a short-term solution.

Our forever home sold in eleven days. We packed up the pieces of our lives into cardboard boxes and plastic tubs. It was numbing, sobering, and devastating. I cried so much during that move that most of the boxes I carried into Tyler's garage were wet with teardrops.

I was grieving over losing River. I was grieving over losing a part of my wife, a part of me, and a part of our kids. And now I was also grieving over losing our home and its millions of joyful memories that had been swallowed up by one really bad one.

I didn't look back as I took the last load up the windy gravel road and past the iron front gate. That sleepy little farm road was where the kids explored, played, and rode bikes, but those visions were now distorted. In what felt like the blink of an eye, that same farm road had become the place where the fire trucks and ambulances screamed their way into my life, tearing open my heart and revealing the worst night of my life.

I haven't been back down that road since.

THE SLIDESHOW

The new home we called our landing pad was helpful, but it wasn't a fix for me. In other words, we might've avoided a massive boulder in the river, but it didn't heal the open wound in my heart. I was never able to settle in there. I may have changed my address by four miles, but the pool never left me.

That's when the visions started.

They tormented me.

I called it my slideshow. It was like walking down the hall of a movie theater where each room was playing the same show on repeat. As I walked through, I would peek in each room and find myself stuck, unable to leave until it was over. I couldn't control it. I couldn't escape it. The same slideshow would explode on the scene in my mind at night before bed, or in the middle of the night, or first thing in the morning, or driving my truck, or even midconversation with someone else. The sequence of the slides could change, but that didn't matter. They were always on a loop.

River is facedown in the pool.

I turn him over, he is purple and limp like a rag doll. Eyes wide and blank. Mouth open and silent.

Amber rushes out to find Riv lifeless in my arms. Panic. Terror.

The sirens, loud and chaotic, ripping through the beautiful farmland.

He's in the hospital bed with breathing tubes in his nose. I open his eyelids. He's not there. His handsome brown eyes are like marbles of emptiness. It's all my fault.

At the funeral he's lying in his red Lightning McQueen casket. Lincoln places his five little fingers on his best friend's box. It leaves a musty imprint that slowly fades away.

As the loop played again and again, my brain searched the

impossible data like a computer trying to access a missing file. Each time the search failed, so it would search again. There had to be a missing link, a piece of forgotten information that completed the narrative to bring order back to the chaos. But it always came up empty. So the search would continue.

The visions were a thief that stole my fatherhood. My manhood. My marriage. My appetite and my sleep. They would burst into my mind and leave me grief-stricken with tears, or angry or embarrassed or frightened, but underlining it all, I was weary and burdened and flat-out exhausted. My arms were tired of rowing against the rough river. I needed help, or else I wasn't going to make it. After several months in the new house, something became painfully obvious. I couldn't run from my nightmares. They had followed me there.

MY ARMS WERE TIRED OF ROWING AGAINST THE ROUGH RIVER.

THE GIFT OF THERAPY

A close friend gifted me and Amber with a solid solution: therapy. I was desperate, and I accepted the offer. We left the kids with their grandmas, jumped on a plane, and flew away for five days with no phones, no Wi-Fi, and no communication with the outside world. We were given no itinerary, no schedule, and absolutely no clue as to what we were getting into besides an airport pickup by a shuttle van that would take us about an hour west to a secluded farm in Tennessee.

I loved it.

I could finally relax.

The accommodations were log cabins and old farmhouses, and the family-style home cooking was served at large picnic tables. Everyone got acquainted rather quickly. We knew we were all so broken and vulnerable that we could comfortably walk up to one another and ask, "Hi! Nice to meet you. So what's your problem?"

Patient: Well, my husband was murdered by a gunman while he walked around the car to let me in the door on our anniversary date night.

Me: Oh, I'm so, so sorry.

Patient: And you?

Me: My son drowned in our home pool fifteen steps away from me and I couldn't revive him.

Patient with teary eyes: Oh my. That must be so difficult. Wanna grab some dinner? They're serving chicken-fried steak.

The facility offered a unique method of therapy with one-on-one sessions by some of the top therapists in the world. Additionally, in the mornings Amber and I would meet in a group with other patients, working together in all sorts of creative activities to help ease the pain and reconcile our emotional torture. The sessions were carefully planned and specifically mapped out to target each individual's story of grief. Our therapist was gentle and kind and patient and deeply empathetic to our story.

One of my personalized sessions was called "brainspotting." It was a technique used on veterans suffering from extreme PTSD. I can explain it something like this.

I was put into a room with low, monotone, droning hypnotic music. Holding a thin telescopic pointer, my therapist would have me stare at the tip of the rod and repeat the story about River's drowning while he took notes. While I was talking, he'd have me pause when I felt any noticeable shifts in my emotional or physical state such as a change in heart rate, compression in the chest, tightness in the stomach, shaky hands, or blurry vision. He was also slowly moving the tip of the pointer right to left and up and down, asking me to report any correlation between my body and emotions in relation to where my eyes connected with the pointer.

This might seem crazy, but what I learned is the basic idea that our brains store specific memories in specific locations. And there's a connection between those specific locations and our map of vision. This explains why when we recite old stories, our eyes will typically look up and to the right, or down and to the left, or anywhere really. Don't believe me? Pay attention the next time your friend tells you a story from the past. They will break eye contact with you and stare off at a spot in the distance as they repeat the story. That's why they call it brainspotting. It's wild stuff.

After reciting the story three or four times from beginning to end, sure enough, there was one spot in my vision where the story had more clarity, more intensity, and more sting. That's where the gruesome memory was stored. Once this was established, we worked to dismantle the slideshow and projector at the core.

Just as I had followed the pinpoint to the spot where I felt the most anxiety, I repeated the process until I found a spot that made me feel the most peace. I located the exact spot on the opposite side of my vision spectrum. This was a happy place where I typically did not allow the memory of River to enter, but we changed that. Locking onto the happy-place spot with my eyes, I forced myself to envision River in my mind. He entered the scene, and I instantly tensed up, but my therapist encouraged me to hang on to it. In this vision, River wasn't in pain. He was smiling and inviting me to follow him. The brainspotting technique allowed me to slowly begin including a happy memory of River in my place of peace where I usually tried to keep him out completely. I began to make an authentic connection in my mind with River in my solitude, which had previously been blocked by trauma. It was intense mental gymnastics, but I genuinely felt better afterward.

ME, THE TREE, AND RIVER

In another exercise, my therapist asked me what or who I wanted to be for my family.

Without hesitation I quipped, "A rock."

He fired back. "And what does a rock lean on?"

I stuttered. I was tongue-tied.

He filled the silence. "I would like you to think of yourself as a tree, not a rock. Maybe a big oak with deep roots that still bends and sways, and occasionally loses branches to weather the storm, but stays upright."

He was suddenly inspired with a new idea and began to elaborate. "In fact," he said, "let's take a few hours and begin a new activity. I want you to grab a piece of paper and a pen and head out into the forest. Find the exact tree that you think represents you. Then sit down and write a conversation that you might have with this tree. Take all the time you need. When you're done, come back and read it to me."

Ahh . . . creative writing. Finally, something I love to do, I thought. Besides, if anything, I could definitely use a hike through the woods to clear my head after all this brainspotting stuff.

It was November and the air was crisp and cool. The sky was overcast and spitting occasional raindrops. There seemed to be an endless variety of trees in the forest. Some were evergreens, and others had lost all their leaves. Most were right in between with shimmering shades of gold, orange, red, and yellow.

The vast variety of fallen leaves became the carpet under my boots as I followed the meandering hills along a slow-moving creek.

And then I found it.

It wasn't the biggest or the most impressive tree in the forest by any stretch, but it was sturdy and youthfully majestic. It was the kind of tree that, if it was in your front yard, would raise the value of your home. It was a nice tree.

I sat down on a stump at the high bank of the creek and began my study. I noticed some of its roots barreled upward into the hill, while others seemed to disappear down into the glistening water below. I pulled out the pen and paper and waited for some kind of earth-shattering inspiration, but nothing came. I was sitting stumped on a stump.

I sat for a few more minutes until it occurred to me that the only practical way to start a conversation with a tree would be the same way I would start a conversation with anyone else—by first introducing myself. This is what I wrote:

Me: Hi, Tree, I'm Granger.

Tree: Hi, Granger.

Me: What is it like to be so tall?

Tree: I can feel the sun before the others, and that's good, but it makes me the most vulnerable to lightning and wind. It's a beautiful risk I take.

Me: I've seen many forests and many much-larger trees than you in my travels.

Tree: I've seen only this forest. Larger trees in other forests don't concern me or matter to me at all.

Me: But the sequoias in California are ancient and incredible! Maybe there's a secret to their life?

LIKE A RIVER

Tree: I only know how to be a red oak in Tennessee.

Me: How deep are your roots?

Tree: As high as my trunk is tall, that's as deep as my roots are buried.

Me: Your roots must be very strong to support your trunk.

Tree: It's not how strong they are. They are as limber and fragile as my limbs. The strength comes from how I bury them in the soil and intertwine with roots from other trees.

Me: Where did the soil come from, and why do you rely on it so much?

Tree: The soil is the history of this forest. It comes from the leaves and seeds and fruit and bark and limbs and roots from the very trees that spawned my acorn and protected me from the wind when I was a sapling. I knew a few of the ancestors that have since fallen here, but most were gone long before my time. All of them contributed to creating the very foundation of what holds me upright.

Me: Why is everyone dropping leaves?

Tree: Because there are seasons when we don't need our leaves. When that season passes, it gives us space to grow new, brighter, and more plentiful leaves.

Me: But some trees have lost more than others. You still have many leaves on top.

Tree: The rate with which we lose them is not important. Any slight breeze or drop of rain can affect some differently than others, but the fact is, we will eventually lose them all. Every last one. And with every leaf we drop to give space for the new, the old is not wasted. They join the others on the ground to perpetuate the soil.

Me: That's cool, Tree. But to be honest, I'm mainly here because of River.

Tree: Me too.

Me: Are you afraid of losing your river?

Tree: The river has brought me life and nutrients that shaped my canopy and helped my limbs spread with incredible nourishment. I am very blessed to be touched by the river because I understand that many red oaks are not. But my strength isn't drawn from the river. It's drawn from the sun. That's why I grow up toward the sky and not down toward the water. I allow the river to feed my growth to the sun, but if I were worried about losing the river, then that would put me and my saplings in danger of losing the light.

Me: I've lost my River. What should I do?

Tree: Shed your dead leaves. Don't hang on to a single one. Drop the burden. New leaves will then have space to grow when the season changes, freeing you of the weight while at the same time preserving the future of your forest. Be thankful that your soil has been enriched by your River along with the fallen leaves and branches of your ancestors. Use your unique soil and the roots of those closest to you to hold you in perfect balance as you keep reaching up, up, up toward the light.

The exercise helped me tremendously that day. For the first time, I was seeing my grief differently and finally beginning to understand that everything in life, even the tragedies, may have a greater purpose for good. However, what held that purpose in balance was still a mystery to me.

MAKING A HOUSE INTO A HOME

After the brainspotting exercise and tree conversation, I was confident that I could maintain some control over my crippling slideshow, but I was still merely a shell of a broken man sitting on a flimsy boat. My therapist lovingly pricked and prodded at all my false securities and fabricated strength, and he uncovered something rather unsettling. I had become addicted to searching real estate apps on my phone for something different from the house we had just moved into.

I wasn't at home yet.

"That habit needs to stop," he said.

I knew he was right, but that didn't change my restless heart. "Tell ya what," he said. "When you get back to Texas, I want you to carry Amber over the threshold of this house and make it a home. Cook meals, invite friends, and make new memories."

I WASN'T AT HOME YET.

It was solid advice.

One week later we returned to Texas. We were home just in time for Thanksgiving and for me to act on all of what I'd learned. But late at night I would slip back into my comforting routine and light up my phone with Zillow or Realtor.com. I'd search and search for anything that made me *feel* at home.

But nothing did.

Not yet.

I missed our ten acres of heaven. I missed the trees and the butterflies and the hummingbirds and the whitetail deer. Most of all, I missed River dashing barefoot through those woods with his wild, red hair.

But that was the past. Just like our little boy, our forever home was dead, and I would never be able to go back there.

Therapy gave me weapons to help me fight against my depression and PTSD. I confidently carried those weapons daily, staying fully aware of the pins and needles under my feet. I was cautious and present in my battle, and I was able to continually mitigate the impact of the slideshow.

By the sixth month after my battle began, I felt as if I had moments when I could finally catch my breath. The current in my river was beginning to settle, and my arms could give the heavy paddling a break—barring any sudden obstacles or turns.

But I was making a severe miscalculation in my ongoing war. I didn't realize it then, but those oars, my weapons, were no more than wooden sticks. The real enemy was looming in the darkness just out of view, silently surrounding my wooden fortress for the final assault. To this enemy, my earthly weapons were powerless.

No, I didn't know it then, but I was falling into a death trap. The horror of the slideshow thus far was feeble compared to the demon I would soon meet face-to-face.

3

THE SHOW MUST GO ON

When you pass through the waters, I will be with you; and through the rivers, they shall not overwhelm you; when you walk through fire you shall not be burned, and the flame shall not consume you.

Isaiah 43:2

I WAS IN THERAPY FIVE months after Riv left us, but I returned to work much sooner than that.

I didn't want to.

I had to.

It's not in my nature to base decisions solely on whether I *want* to do something; rather, I base them on their importance to my life and the lives of others. God willing, one day I hope to be able to look back and see that my life was measured not by the decisions that made me feel happy or comfortable but by the ones that mattered. For instance, none of us go to a funeral because it makes us feel happy; we go because it's important. It matters.

Sometimes the choices that matter are *very* uncomfortable. That's probably an understatement as it relates to my summer of 2019.

After we lost Riv, I stayed home for three weeks before the next decision became imminent. All I wanted to do was curl up and hide away like a spider in a dark cave, but the decision broke down like this.

- **I had thirteen men on salary.** No matter how much water is in the bathtub, when the faucet is turned off and the drain is open, the water quickly empties out. All these men had families and livelihoods that depended on my touring, and the loyalty they'd shown over the years was very important to me.
- **I needed to get out of that town.** I needed a distraction and some sense of normalcy. I'm not great at multitasking, and for me, performing onstage takes a lot of presence of

mind. Many people return to work in the midst of grief for this very reason. I decided it would be best to take Amber and the two kids with me on the bus so that we could all be distracted together.

- **I had a lot of eyes on me, and I felt the weight of that.** You'll probably read that and think, *No, Granger, your family is the only thing that matters in the wake of this tragedy.* You're not wrong, but let me explain.

YOUR STORY MATTERS

In the hospital, when the doctors told us that River wasn't going to survive his injury, we were overwhelmed with shock. It was the kind of shock that was so devastating that I couldn't cry (even though the doctor did when he delivered the news). Maybe I had already run out of tears. Maybe I was so numb that my body had surged into fight-or-flight mode just to keep my own heart beating.

Amber and I slowly walked the hall back to River's hospital room and laid our hands on him. The room was a mess between duffel bags, blankets, pillows, and flowers. I'd slept on the couch the previous night, and Amber had slept in the bed with Riv. We didn't really sleep, but you know what I mean. That's where we laid our heads amid the busy nurse interruptions and the relentless *beep . . . beep . . . beep* of the heart monitor that was occasionally interrupted by some kind of low oxygen, low blood pressure, seizure, or other piercing alarm that jolted us upright throughout the night and day. The room was a wreck, except one thing. River. He was perfect. Neatly tucked into his favorite blue blanket, beautiful red hair swooped to the side, rosy cheeks, and the fingers of his left hand wrapped around his favorite, scuffed up #95 Lightning McQueen Hot Wheels car.

In that numbing moment, with our hands laid on our precious boy, Amber looked at me with such intensity, such clarity, and said something so confidently that it caught me off guard: "I want to donate his organs." Then she began to softly cry again, "His little body is perfect, flawless. It's only his brain that's damaged. Surely there are people in the world who could use this tragedy as their miracle." Later, after some clarity on the moment, Amber admitted that those words must have been God-breathed and not her own intuition.

Regardless of the inspiration, those words changed the trajectory of our grief. Suddenly, through our darkest day, there was a light. It was very faint, but we could see it. This tragedy was *not* totally meaningless.

SUDDENLY, THROUGH OUR DARKEST DAY, THERE WAS A LIGHT.

This was no turnkey solution to our pain. In fact, in many ways, this decision made it even more difficult. The doctors told us that if we wanted to donate his organs, it would prolong the inevitable, his death, by at least twenty-four hours. And it was risky. Donor recipients would need to be located through a worldwide search, and if River went brain dead before they were matched, it would change the recipient qualifications. His body would need to be injected continually with more medications to prolong his life—meds like epinephrine and norepinephrine to keep his blood pressure up, fentanyl for perceived pain, and others to reduce his seizures along with sedatives to help monitor his neurological activity. All of this pumped through IVs into a seemingly healthy boy who just a day earlier was hysterically laughing while he dumped stale popcorn out of a backpack onto the living-room couch.

A new group of surgeons joined us from a different wing of the hospital and explained the new plan. In a race against the clock, a team would locate viable recipients and then transport River to the operating room. From there we would say our last goodbyes; they would turn off life support, allow his heart to stop beating on its own, and begin the retrieval surgery.

It was heart-wrenching stuff and the kind of information that was nearly impossible to comprehend as a father.

"Okay. Yessir. Yes, ma'am. I understand."

That was about the extent of my muttering to the doctors.

We waited. We prayed. We talked to Riv. We cried. We welcomed family and friends into the room to say their goodbyes to the beautiful, little, wild boy. And then we waited and prayed again.

No eating.

No sleeping.

The incredible nurses at the hospital would frequent the room and adjust blankets and administer new meds, all the while talking to River as if he were fully aware of their calm voices.

"Okay, sweet boy, I'm going to adjust your pillow right quick. Sorry if my hands are a little chilly."

And then, finally, at about 11:00 a.m. the following day, the news came: it was time.

We wheeled his bed out into the hallway for his last earthly journey, and I paused.

"Hey, everyone," I choked up, talking to the group. "Everything Riv did in his life was at full speed. He loved going *fast*—whether on bare feet or wheels. Can we give him one more ride and push him really fast down this hall? That's what he would want."

The doctors and nurses all broke open in wide, heartfelt grins. "Okay, y'all," one announced. "Listen up! We're going to give River one last ride. Let's push him *fast*!"

It was only about one hundred paces, but I smiled through my tears for the first time in two days as we raced our boy past room after room of onlooking doctors, nurses, family, friends, and other residents who rallied in passionate cheers. I'm pretty confident River set a speed record on a hospital bed that day that still stands in the state of Texas.

When we arrived outside the operating room, Amber and I kissed his face one last time, they pushed him in, and the double doors swung to a close. I stared blankly at the gray surgery door. I repeated the mantra to myself, "You saved lives today, Riv. Your story matters."

IT WASN'T MEANINGLESS

Before I made the decision to go back out on the road and face the world, Amber and I, with the help of my brother (and manager) Tyler and my publicists, Nicole and Jay, decided to refuse all media interviews of any kind. It seemed like every TV show and radio station in the country wanted to cover the news, but frankly, we just didn't know who to trust with the sensitive story, and we wanted to protect our children, especially Lincoln and his involvement with the water gun fight. He had already been questioned alone several times by Child Protective Services and asked over and over to repeat exactly what he saw by the pool. I was a grown man who could take some heavy blows as a failed parent, but not our innocent five-year-old boy.

We decided to speak to the public in one location, in one video, on our family YouTube channel, The Smiths. We walked into the woods to River's favorite spot, where he had played with his toy tractors in the dirt, and turned on the camera. We spoke candidly and unrehearsed. Our message was pretty simple: We were beyond hurt. We were in a world of grief, but we would be relentless in looking for meaning in this dark time.

The organ donation was the catalyst of that discovery. Next, we raised money for the hospital through River T-shirt sales. That was the least we could do in exchange for the grace that those doctors and nurses showed us in our time of great despair. Finally (and what ultimately led me back to the road) came our desire to live out our grief journey publicly.

WE WERE IN A WORLD OF GRIEF, BUT WE WOULD BE RELENTLESS IN LOOKING FOR MEANING IN THIS DARK TIME.

There were a lot of eyes on me. I could have disappeared into my spider cave, and most people probably wouldn't have blamed me for it. But among those eyes were a bunch of hurting people. Grieving people. People without hope, stuck in perpetual limbo from their own experience with loss.

I'm not strong enough to proclaim that I was able to sidestep my own suffering for the sake of others. In fact, it's pretty much the opposite. I was able to somewhat alleviate my own pain by showing other grieving families that I would continue to press forward through the fire. I wouldn't be without burns, but I refused to stand still, for the sake of those watching and those desperately hoping for a path out of the flames. It wasn't much, but at least it was a forward direction, and I was going to cling to even the smallest bit of relief.

Back then, I had no idea just how hard my path out of the flames would be.

FAKING IT

The next string of shows on the books after my three weeks of cancellations was in the Midwest. We piled into my bus, and left Texas and our home.

I can still see the evidence of that tour from photos on my phone. We smiled, ate good food, nursed a baby kangaroo and carried it around in a cloth sack, and Lincoln and I played a lot of baseball. But I was faking it all. I suppressed the slideshow looping in my mind, along with all the terrifying memories, and kept moving forward. I worked really hard to stay present and to keep paddling my boat down the raging river. A full day was too much to handle. Honestly, a full hour was too much to handle, so I lived minute to minute. Sometimes breath to breath. And if a breath was too much of a burden, I managed my pain one heartbeat at a time.

The shows themselves were a blur. I forgot words and chords to my most popular songs. I lied with every smile.

The first concert back was the most difficult show of my life. It was June 22, 2019, in Camdenton, Missouri, but it might as well have been Camdenton, Misery. Not because of the people but because of where I was in my head.

The concert was in a large outdoor pavilion with several thousand in attendance. My heart pounded as I stood in the wing behind the curtain while my band began to play our first song. I internalized the whole situation.

They are waiting to watch the train wreck. They're hitting the brakes so they can witness a broken man burn publicly—like a flame-engulfed truck turned over on I-35.

My thoughts continued to get deeper and darker.

They came here for one reason, to watch the public display of a father who failed at his only job—keeping his son alive. I am now best known as the man who killed his son.

Truth be told, those were my own insecurities attacking me. In reality, peppered throughout the pavilion were hundreds of red River T-shirts, the ones we sold to benefit the hospital. Bless their hearts. They stood. They cried. They were patient with my stumbling, mumbling, shaky voice, and missed chords. They showed me with their misty eyes that River's life mattered to them too.

It's interesting to me as I write this book that some of you reading this were likely there in the crowd in Camdenton and the shows that followed. Maybe you were expecting more emotion from me. Maybe you were inspired by my perceived strength after tragedy. Maybe you didn't even notice a difference.

It was all a facade. It was a performance in every sense of the word, but it felt more like pretending.

I've been a professional performer for most of my life, but that was some of the best pretending I've ever done. By the final song each night, I could barely hold back the heavy tears ready to erupt from my eyes.

Afterward, I would make a beeline straight to the back bedroom of Wildflower and completely break down. What a wretch I was. How could I sell tickets, squeeze out fake smiles, and receive audience cheers just weeks after burying our innocent child? My breakdown was accompanied by the crippling guilt from my seemingly obvious lack of supervision that led to River getting inside the gate. Then the paralyzing slideshow would begin again. These thought-loops ravaged me.

My band and crew felt it too. If anyone saw through my pretending, it was those guys. Most have toured with me for over a decade. They were there when we announced the River pregnancy and all his birthdays. Only a month earlier River was on tour with us, always the life and laugh of the party. They also came to the hospital on his last day and attended his funeral. They knew

I was pretending. My bus drivers superglued Lightning McQueen cars to the dashboards just like the one I carried in my blue jeans pocket. The sound crew put them on their audio consoles. (Those toy cars are still there today.)

Each night we played one of my songs called “Heaven Bound Balloons.” My monitor engineer, Will, would remove his hat and get choked up each and every night, and although I never acknowledged it with words, the audience knew I was singing every line of that song about River.

But even that was pretending.

It was an audience distraction.

A magician’s sleight of hand.

It was the more unsuspecting song of mine called “You’re in It” that leveled me each night. It was Riv’s favorite song, the one he belted out nightly in our kitchen with a kid-sized guitar strapped around his shoulders while doing some kind of hip-thrusting dance move that would make even Elvis himself blush.

Of course, like everything else, I didn’t tell anyone that I could barely make it through that song without crying (and I even skipped it on the set list several nights), because I didn’t want to call more attention to my brokenness.

I hated touring in 2019.

All of it.

I even played an incredible bucket list show with one of my heroes, Garth Brooks, in Boise, Idaho, on the Smurf Turf at Boise State University. Garth found me backstage and with tears on his cheeks gave me a warm hug. “I have no idea how you’re even standing up straight, brother,” Garth whispered in empathy in a way that only Garth can. “I don’t even know why you took this show.” He made an excellent point.

Night after night I found myself counting down songs on the set list.

Nine more 'til I'm done.

Eight more.

Well, eight and one-half because I'm only into verse two of this terrible song. When will it be over?!

When the grueling set would finally end, I wouldn't talk to anyone. I'd go straight to the shower and then straight to bed.

But no one in the audience perceived any of this.

THE LIE

I'm pretty certain that if you had seen me during the summer of 2019, you would've said I was doing "pretty good," all things considered.

My clothes were washed, and my hair was combed. I remembered to brush my teeth and occasionally slap a splash of cologne on my neck. I smiled and nodded and looked people in the eye as they stumbled over their sincere condolences in nearly every conversation I had in meet and greets, airports, parks, shopping malls, gas stations, and grocery stores. To the audience, the rhythm and flow of my shows must have felt seemingly normal again as I became more and more numb to the new reality of being viewed as the father who had lost a son to drowning.

My Instagram and Facebook posts were professional, well-lit photos with lengthy, heartfelt captions, and they were sometimes even a bit misleading to distract from the truth of the only thing that was really on my mind. Those posts are still up. For example:

> Right before we walked on stage tonight, Jonny asked me, "Remember the 1st time I played bass with you? 10 years ago in Webster TX and there were 40 people."

> Yep, of course. I remember all the shows. How could I not? I've played shows where I broke ribs and punctured my lung, played for important suits in DC and heroes in Iraq. I've seen country kids in the mud in Iowa and cowboy hats in Australia. I've dislocated shoulders at county fairs and grabbed some forehead stitches in College Station. I've played a few times for a lot of people and many times for a few people. I've played shows at the greatest times of my life and I've played shows after terrible loss, again and again. And that's my job. But through it all, it's the people that keep me coming back. If you've seen me lately, please let me say thank you for the support. Through it all. Seriously, you're the fuel to my flame . . . still. I can feel the love.[1]

In reality I wanted to delete social media and quit music for the rest of my life. Maybe that spider cave was a better idea after all.

THE TRUTH IS, EVERYONE IS HURTING FROM SOMETHING—EVEN THE PEOPLE YOU THINK HAVE IT ALL TOGETHER.

Why does social media enthrall us so much? Don't we know from my story and countless others that it's all a lie? We *only* post things the way we *want* everyone else to perceive it. Sure, it can be lined in truth, but we still pick only the best photo with the best lighting from our best side. We edit the caption and then edit it again until it reads exactly like what we hope everyone believes about us.

The stage is no different. The five-foot-high risers, lights, haze, and loud music all just perpetuate the performance—the pretending.

Let me go even further. Life is a stage for all of us. At some level, we're all performing on it all the time; but the truth is, everyone is hurting from something—even the people you think have it all together.

I was completely unraveling, and my boat was sinking, but no one knew how deep I had already gone.

If I fooled you in 2019, shame on me for that. I would soon pay a hefty price for not acknowledging my pain and struggles. The storm continued raging. The dam to my pretty little lake had an irreparable crack, and the river was rising.

4

WHEN SELF-HELP STOPS HELPING

The king's heart is a stream of water
in the hand of the Lord;
he turns it wherever he will.
Proverbs 21:1

I'VE ALWAYS BEEN A BIT eccentric. Maybe that's an understatement, or maybe *passionate* is a better word because if I'm going to do something, I'll do it to the extreme. Even to a fault.

I'm so passionate that when I decided to be a country music singer, and I didn't have much talent at songwriting or singing, playing guitar, or standing in front of large crowds, I pushed on through because I loved the idea of it more than I was terrified by it. I just kept on through the lack of talent without ever devising a plan B. I endured the endless highway miles in a pickup truck, then a Suburban, and eventually a fifteen-passenger van. Years went by without gaining any real fans. In fact, there were countless nights when we played a concert for the bartender. One time, the father of one of my friends from high school cornered me and asked, "Hey, man, this music thing; when's it gonna give? When will you get a real job?"

As I was growing up, my parents gave me three very valuable gifts: my name, braces for my teeth, and the blessing to chase this crazy dream. They believed in me when no one else did.

If I'm passionate enough—actually, let's just call it what it is, stubborn—to last fifteen years in that kind of ego-sucking vacuum before I ever got my first tour bus in 2013, then you can imagine how easily I latched on to the self-help movement. As I shared in the first chapter, armed with a little self-determination, self-discipline, and self-motivation, I swallowed the idea hook, line, and sinker. And I bit deep.

FALLING OFF THE STAGE

My plunge into self-help actually started in December 2017 when I fell off a stage in New Jersey. It happened in a music venue called Starland Ballroom while I was performing an acoustic concert for a packed house. I stepped on a floor monitor that was balancing halfway off the edge of the deck. When I shifted my weight, it tumbled forward, and I came spiraling down off the front of the stage along with it. I landed on my back on top of the V-shaped speaker and heard a loud *crack*. The crowd gasped as I immediately sprung up and bellied my way back onto the stage. Totally embarrassed, I smiled, waved to the crowd, and mouthed, "I'm okay."

But I wasn't.

I strolled up to the mic to tell some kind of joke to break the ice with all the wide-eyed patrons, but nothing came out of my mouth. There was no air in my lungs, and worse than that, I felt an agonizing crunch happening somewhere in my back.

Without losing a smile, and the band never missing a beat, I yanked the mic off the stand and spun it around to let the crowd sing "Backroad Song" back to me.

In the wings, my horrified tour manager, Chris, was standing at the ready signaling, "*You good?*"

I shook him off nonchalantly, "*No*."

When the song was over, I went straight from the stage into an Uber to be hurried off to the emergency room, still just barely sucking air out of my deflated lungs.

The X-ray was no surprise. It showed two completely broken ribs just to the left of my spine. Soon after my diagnosis, however, I did get a surprise from the doctors. Apparently after reexamining the X-rays, they noticed I had a punctured lung that was leaking fluid into my chest cavity. That called for more serious medical action. The ER tech called an ambulance; they put me into a precautionary neck brace, strapped me to the fold-up bed, and carted me across town to another hospital.

When we arrived, a slew of doctors put me on a table with blinding lights, injected me with morphine, and used scissors to cut off all my clothes. They poked, prodded, flipped me over, and X-rayed me again to discover that the fluid leak didn't require cutting open my chest.

The only thing to do was wait six weeks for my body to heal itself. They set me up in a room, but I was adamant to get out of there as soon as possible and on a flight bound for Texas. I arrived a few thousand miles of agitating air bumps later. Amber picked me up, took me home, and propped me up with pillows on our living room couch, and there I sat.

WHAT WOULD TOM BRADY DO?

Six weeks.

It was an impossible task for a busybody like me to sit still. For the first time in many years, my calendar was cleared; and for a month and a half, I had absolutely nothing to do besides trade out the ice packs and heating pads and build up my lung strength with a spirometer.

I asked myself, "*What would Tom Brady do?*"

This seemed like a common quarterback injury, and I desperately wanted to know what an elite athlete would do to help speed up recovery. I picked up the TV remote and turned on YouTube and Netflix, looking for healing hacks.

I watched for weeks.

I learned about medications and meditations, ice baths, cryotherapy, and steam rooms. I watched countless documentaries about veggie juicing and body cleansing and the dangers of processed foods, GMOs, and plastic in the oceans, and every other dramatic, oversensitized, "world is ending," self-funded film on the internet. The world set its trap, and I got snared.

I was pouring kale into blenders and dipping into my freezing cold swimming pool with a stopwatch. I was choking down horse pill–sized vitamins from Amazon and clearing my head with East Asian mindfulness apps on my phone.

That's when I found Tony Robbins.

Tony was doing all that stuff and seemed to give people the perfect advice through any kind of unique suffering that life threw at them. Held captive on my couch, I watched every seminar and read every book available from Tony.

MY MORNING ROUTINE

A few months later, after a full recovery, my self-help craze intensified. I will never forget the book that helped me turn that corner.

It was 2018 when my little brother, Parker, gave me a book ironically titled *The Miracle Morning* by Hal Elrod. "Read it," he said. "You'll love it."

I did.

And he was right.

It was a self-help book written by a man who was in a major car wreck, sustained serious injuries, and came out on the other side with a refreshed, rejuvenated outlook on life. Similar to my rib-breaking accident but with far worse injuries.

The author drove home the importance of a morning routine to jump-start each day, which would lead to a happier, more fulfilling life. The ritualistic steps were spelled out with the acronym SAVERS.

Silence
Affirmations
Visualizations
Exercise
Reading
Scribing

The book didn't reveal anything new that I hadn't already learned during my Tony Robbins phase, but it did help me organize my activities into specific time blocks in the morning so that by 9:00 a.m. all my personal development was finished for the day. I raced through the book and could barely wait to put the new routine into action. I followed every last word like a lost sheep chasing a shepherd. My personalized schedule looked something like this:

5:00 a.m.: Alarm goes off, no snoozing. Brush teeth. Get dressed. Make coffee. Go to my studio office.

5:30–5:40 a.m.: Mindfulness. I used the guided meditation app Ten Percent Happier.

5:40–5:50 a.m.: I read a Christian 365-day devotional page. I had many different kinds.

5:50–6:00 a.m.: I wrote down a list of things that made me feel grateful. Then I wrote a gratitude letter to someone in my life who was important to me and mailed it later.

6:00–6:10 a.m.: I made a power list of the top things that needed to get done that day, no more than five items, starting with the most important down to the least important. I checked off the list during the course of each day.

6:10–6:20 a.m.: I worked on my long-term vision board, mainly concerning my apparel company, Yee Yee, and my music career.

6:20–6:30 a.m.: I journaled the events in my life. I used an app called Day One. (I still have all of those entries.)

6:30–7:30 a.m.: I went to the gym for strength training. Each day of the week was a different muscle group. This part wasn't new for me, so it was an easy morning inclusion. On the way to and from the gym, I listened to an audiobook or podcast. There are sixty-seven completed audiobooks on my phone from that era alone. I soon decided that every time I was in my truck, at any time of day, I wouldn't lose myself in mindless channel surfing; instead, I would only listen to some form of educational or work-related audio.

7:45 a.m.: I was back home either playing with River and seeing the kids off to school or taking them to school myself. I made a protein shake with two scoops of protein powder, two scoops of green superfood powder, frozen kale, one apple, one banana, carrots, almonds (or natural peanut butter), water, and ice. After that I would read ten pages of a nonfiction personal development or life skill book, different from the audiobook I listened to in the truck. (Fiction reading was for bedtime only.) Then I worked on learning Spanish with language apps and videos.

9:00 a.m.: It was now time to begin carving away at the five items on my power list.

Late afternoons and evenings were "scheduled" for Amber and the kids, midday was for music and media interviews, but my morning was all mine. I loved it.

AN UNUSUAL ADDICTION

Give or take a trip to the gym, I followed this routine every day. I made it happen in my studio, on airplanes, in terminals, in hotel rooms, and on my tour bus. I did it on Christmas morning and on vacation. I craved it. I lived for it. I became addicted to it.

Self-help is very addictive, by the way. Maybe it's the ego trip that perpetuates it. I mean, the term *self-help* begins with the word *self.* There's a prideful idea that says, "Wow! Look at all this stuff I've done this morning while the rest of the world is too lazy to even get out of bed!"

I hope you're hearing how ridiculous that sounds. I hope you're imagining how robotic I was, because there's a good point to the story that I want to show you. But first, I want to tell you how I took all this self-help to an even more extreme level.

After several months, when this routine wasn't enough of a challenge for me, I added more layers. By early 2019 I wanted to do something each day that was difficult for me mentally, so I racked my brain for what that could be.

Running.

I hate running. I'm one of those guys who proudly proclaims, "Oh, I'm a sprinter, not a long-distance runner."

Between stage performances, cardio, and weightlifting, I didn't *need* any more exercise, but I decided to add running to my daily routine, just for the mental stamina. I dreaded doing it, but by adding it, I could look at any difficulties that arose and say with confidence, "Well, I've already tackled one thing today that really challenges me, so I'll be just fine with this new problem."

My running rules were simple:

1. never skip a day
2. outdoors only
3. minimum two miles

Maybe the rules were simple, but the execution wasn't. Some days I was in an airplane most of the day, landed, went straight to the venue, played a concert, and then had to run at midnight when all I wanted to do was sleep. Some days it was pouring rain. I ran in North Dakota one time in zero degrees and blizzard conditions. For the record, I never learned to enjoy it, but that was kind of the point. If I actually liked it, I would need to switch to something uncomfortable again.

I was all about steering my own boat on the river so if the river changed course suddenly, I could redirect my own path. It was an adversity defense tactic. It was false security. It was putting my trust in my own power, and it ended up being a huge problem.

During this time, I also drastically monitored my eating. I downloaded an app called MyFitnessPal and began tracking everything that went into my body. I set my water consumption and macro goals (carbs, fats, proteins) for my daily eating and drinking and met those goals precisely—nothing over, nothing under.

I carried a dietary scale with me everywhere and weighed oatmeal, broccoli, rice, turkey breast—whatever made it to my plate had to first sit on that scale. The app itself has a database of almost every brand name food and generic vegetable that helped me quickly identify the macros. If it didn't fit my plan, I didn't eat it.

I remember being in Louisiana, and hospitality brought our crew homemade chicken gumbo that looked and smelled amazing. I filled a bowl, then sat down at the table to measure and do the math. Nope. That gumbo would put my fats over my daily count. I walked back and dumped the bowl back into the pot. My guitar player, Todd, stared at me speechless, like I had completely lost my mind. He was correct; I had.

Why in the world was I doing all this? I started slow and built habits, but then the habits became addictions.

RECOGNIZING THE PROBLEM

I need to clarify that most of what I was doing was good for me. There are *far worse* habits to make. In fact, I can say the same thing for almost the entire self-help industry. It's good stuff! So no, let's not start burning the self-help books—keep 'em. And things like self-discipline, setting family and business goals, gratitude, healthy eating, exercise, mindfulness over distractions, reading books instead of scrolling TikTok, those are some great things to practice in life.

But here's the problem—I thought I was building a solid dam, but life is like a river that can't be contained. I wish I hadn't learned this the hard way, but I'm sharing my story so that maybe you don't.

I THOUGHT I WAS BUILDING A SOLID DAM, BUT LIFE IS LIKE A RIVER THAT CAN'T BE CONTAINED.

There I was controlling my finances and my body and my health and my sleep and my family and my eyes and my ears and my songs and my radio dial. Maybe I was preparing myself in case of another rib injury or worse. Maybe I was recognizing my own fragile mortality and desperately trying to live as much of my maximum "in the moment" potential as possible. Maybe I didn't want to look back on my life and regret not making the most of it.

Ahh, yes. It was all those things and more. I wish I could talk to that version of myself.

I'd shake him up a little bit with the truth.

I was attempting to manipulate my river, trimming the overlying branches, pulling out the stumps, and removing the boulders. I was bricking the banks and damming up the widest spots to prevent flooding.

But I had completely overlooked the most important thing.

Although we can pretend to contain our piece of waterfront, we can't control the power of the river itself. That comes from the Source. And until we finally connect with the Source of the river, everything done downstream is useless and therefore powerless to make a difference.

DROWNING IN THE FLOOD

This is who I was at 7:30 p.m. on June 4, 2019.

I remember our first night home after the funeral, lying in bed, squinting at the dark bedroom ceiling. Our baby boy—the one we had coddled, and fed, and taught to walk and talk, and protected with sunscreen and bug spray and vitamins; the boy we had told to slow down on his go-kart, wash the mud off his hands, put on a rain jacket, and wipe the chocolate ice cream off his face; the one we had prayed with, kissed, and tucked into bed every single night—was now one hundred miles away in a secluded country cemetery with six feet of dirt on top of him. How could a parent take one more breath knowing that?

Ignoring the elusive sleep, or lack thereof, I still set my alarm and did the one thing I knew how to do in adversity—my miracle morning routine. But the meditation and mindfulness only made more headspace for the dreaded slideshow and certainly didn't leave me "ten percent happier."

My Christian devotional had become gibberish and unfulfilling. What could I write in my gratefulness journal?

At least my other two kids are alive?

Erase.

At least my wife hasn't divorced me yet for drowning her baby?

No. Erase. Bad idea.

My power list consisted of (1) survive one day and (2) drink water so your tears don't dehydrate you. My long-term vision board's biggest vision was, I'll probably quit music.

Journal? There's no way I want to remember this day, so I didn't write anything.

I didn't read. Didn't go on a run. Our beautiful family and neighbors brought us meals, so I just ate whatever was there if I was hungry. I didn't measure anything.

I still went to the gym, but instead of listening to an audiobook on the way, I drove in silence. That was my first public appearance, and I felt like every eye in the gym was on me. I didn't speak to anyone, and no one spoke to me besides some friends lovingly encouraging me on my bench press. When I got back to my truck, I cried again.

Broken.

I'm the kind of guy who probably wouldn't win very many bar fights. In fact, I don't think I've ever won any. But I'm also the guy who's stubborn enough to keep getting back up after every knockdown. That's me. I've survived Texas high school football two-a-days in August, the Corps of Cadets at Texas A&M, five consecutive annual one-hundred-mile walks in five days for the troops after my entertainment tours in Iraq, and multiple stage injuries while still finishing every show.

Look, the point I'm trying to make is this: I consider myself a mentally tough person. Whether it's patience, fatigue, no sleep, physical pain, or emotional stress, I can press forward through all of that with the best of 'em. The only reason I'm emphasizing that is because I want you to know the extent of the force of the flood that finally broke me.

I couldn't fix this in my own strength.

Just like my boy River, I was drowning. And I had no idea where to go for air.

5

WHAT MY DAD TAUGHT ME

You visit the earth and water it; you greatly enrich it; the river of God is full of water; you provide their grain, for so you have prepared it.

Psalm 65:9

I HAVEN'T EATEN TAKE-AND-BAKE PIZZA in eight years and fifty-six days. How do I know that exact date? Because that's the food I was eating when Mom called with one of the hardest phone calls I've ever received. It went exactly like this:

Me: Hello?

Mom: Granger, what are you doing right now?

Me: Oh, I'm just eating take-and-bake pizza.

Mom: Are you alone, or are you with family?

Me: I'm with the family. What's up?

Mom: (long pause) Your dad had a heart attack. And he died.

My battle to move forward after losing River was numbing, overwhelming, and seemingly impossible; but at its core, the emotional destruction of grief wasn't new for me.

Sometimes I replay in my head that sequence of words from the conversation with my mom in 2014 because it's so surreal, like a dream. But I wasn't dreaming, and it was very real. A few hours earlier Mom was with us. She was visiting for a few days and enjoying our brand-new two-month-old baby boy, Lincoln. When she returned home that Wednesday at 6:40 p.m., all the lights in the house were off, and Dad wasn't there to greet her at the door. Our yellow lab, Rio, was stumbling around anxiously in the dark as Mom set down her suitcase and called for him.

When she went back to the bedroom, she found him in his chair, eyes closed and chin down like he was sleeping, but she knew he wasn't.

We have minimal clues about what happened in the minutes

leading up to his massive heart attack. He was in his chair, and there was a small towel on the table next to him. Outside in the grass was a weed trimmer and a chainsaw with the engine casing opened and a screwdriver lying next to it. Typical tools of an early spring day's work. His phone was still in the kitchen plugged into the charger, and there were trash bags that he had not yet taken to the gate, like he typically did on Wednesday mornings.

Dad was sixty-one years old and not exactly in peak shape physically, but he didn't have any prior symptoms or reasons for alarm. He was stubborn and didn't visit a doctor routinely. I'm assuming that if he had, they would've found a 99 percent artery blockage and performed immediate open-heart surgery, just like his dad had two separate times and his older brother once. I'm certainly not a doctor, so that's only speculation from a grieving son who was searching for some kind of explanation to it all.

As I struggled to process the information on that phone call with Mom, the next step became even more upsetting. She asked me to tell my two younger brothers.

Tyler, my middle brother, lived a few streets over, so I asked him to meet me at my house. As soon as he came in and saw my face, he instantly knew that this was a bad day. Through my tears and shortness of breath, I told him the minimal information that I knew.

Tyler immediately reacted with denial and confusion, which quickly settled into hurt and sadness. My next call would be more difficult because I wouldn't be face-to-face to soften the impact.

I thought about my youngest brother, Parker. He was twenty years old, attending Texas A&M University in College Station. He was a sophomore in the Corps of Cadets and was responsible for the school mascot, an American collie named Reveille. He was waiting in the drive-through line with friends at Whataburger when I called him.

"Hey, can you call me back when you're out of the car and alone?" I asked in a low tone.

In those brief moments my heart ached for Parker. He wasn't fatherless yet—not until I would make that a reality for him. I wanted to delay it. I wanted to let him have a few more minutes in a world where our loving father was still alive and still available to talk with for advice, for teaching, for encouraging, or just for listening. Only a few minutes after receiving the worst phone call from Mom, I delivered the worst phone call to Dad's youngest son.

As a family, we mustered composure, packed up the car, and made the two-hour drive to Mom. The next few days were rough.

A hazy fog.

Funeral arrangements and announcements would be exhausting for anyone in a clear mind, but sadly, no one is in a clear mind in the early stages of grief. We comforted Mom, tackled the many logistical duties, busied ourselves with ranch work, and grieved the absence of our leader.

HEARSES DON'T PULL TRAILERS

The reality of our mortality and the thief of life become real in these moments.

It's common to hear the saying "You never see a U-Haul trailer behind a hearse." Which means, of course, that you don't take anything with you when you leave this earth. It was a strange feeling thumbing through Dad's wallet. He left his driver's license, his credit card, a few bills of cash, and a local septic company's business card among other things. He left his Texas A&M class ring and his Casio G-Shock watch. He left his reading glasses and his favorite snapback trucker cap. He left his pickup truck in the driveway. He even left his wedding band.

How could a man go anywhere without these things? He wasn't coming back for any of it, and he certainly didn't need them where he was going. In my long moments of wondering, I thought about what I might leave for people in the dark corners of my physical existence. I guess that's a good question that we should continue to ask ourselves. What would make a difference to those left behind? What wouldn't?

What we found in Dad's closet, in his blue jeans pockets, wasn't a surprise. It was what we found tucked deep in his desk drawer that caught us off guard. I don't remember why we were rummaging through that desk—we were probably looking for some kind of paperwork, medical record, or passcode that we needed—but that's where we found the poem. It was old, faded, tattered on the edges, and handwritten in Dad's unique handwriting. This is how it read:

> To laugh often and much;
> To win the respect of intelligent people
> and the affection of children;
> To earn the appreciation of honest critics
> and endure the betrayal of false friends;
> To appreciate beauty;
> To find the best in others;
> To leave the world a bit better, whether by
> a healthy child, a garden patch
> or a redeemed social condition;
> To know even one life has breathed
> easier because you have lived;
> This is to have succeeded.[2]

It was the first time my brothers or I had ever seen that poem. Dad never mentioned it to anyone. At some point in his life he read it and took it upon himself to write it out and keep it in his desk. We'll never know the exact inspiration behind it all, but I often envision what that moment was like for him and why he was so moved by it.

It honestly doesn't take a lot of imagination, because in his life, Dad embodied every word in that poem to a T. Also, it was just like him to discover it, write it, memorize it, store it away, live it, and not ever mention it to another human being. It wouldn't have been his style to brag about it like some righteous Kool-Aid that he was drinking.

It blew me away thinking that, after all his years, he was still teaching and showing me how to be a man, even after his death.

Maybe more importantly, his final lesson was teaching me how to grieve. But there's more.

Somewhere in the group of scattered pages in the desk was something else that caught my eye. It was a job résumé. We didn't know that Dad was applying for another job at the time, but that wasn't the big deal. The big deal was what he wrote on the first line of the résumé. But before I tell you that, you'll need to know who he was.

AN UNASSUMING, POOR RANCHER

Dad was a poor rancher in Texas.

Well, that's not exactly accurate, but that's what you might've thought if you had seen him sitting in his clunky 1974 GMC pickup at the one stoplight in Clifton, Texas. He would chuckle and call the truck "two-tone." What that meant was that one tone was faded olive green and the other was gray Bondo paint that he'd used to hide the dents and scuffs. The rusty roof was wrinkled like an old, smashed Coke can because one time when

I was a teenager, I turned it over on a cattle panel fence. (It may be an important footnote that no one, not even me, was actually *in* the truck when it flipped. I had left it in Neutral and forgot to put on the emergency brake. A stiff breeze came from nowhere and pushed it down a hill and over the fence. Probably not my proudest moment.)

The most notable characteristic of this truck was likely the missing driver's side door. (Once again, another idiotic teenage mishap by yours truly.)

You couldn't miss this pickup in such a small town. Despite the noisy, broken muffler, the off-timed backfiring straight-six engine, the rusted paint, or even the missing door, Dad had a strange confidence driving that old relic. He paid $1,100 for it in 1996, and you would've thought that he had brought home a Porsche by the way he beamed behind the sunburned steering wheel.

To Mom's embarrassment, the missing door of the old truck fully exposed the even bigger relic in this stereotypical redneck postcard imagery, and that was Dad himself. Imagine this six-foot-three, 220-pound teddy bear with uncombed white hair flipping out of a sweat-ringed feedstore trucker cap. His hands and forearms were always scraped and bloody from whatever thorny vegetation he was tearing into that day. His shirts had tiny burn holes from rogue brushfire embers, and his pants were repaired and patched, sewn by his own hands and tucked into the tops of his twenty-year-old Red Wing boots. Dad was a sight. In fact, if it weren't for Mom's grace and her ever-so-loving encouragement—let's just say she was the only reason that he didn't become a complete Texas caveman.

After that description of him I bet you think you have Dad pegged. But that's not at all the whole story about him. You see, Dad was good at a lot of things, but he was *great* at raising men.

Dad influenced so many people's lives, but none as much as my own. Without him I would be half the man I am today. Let me explain.

STUDS VS. DUDS

He wasn't always the redneck rancher I've described. I remember my dad wearing a suit to work for most of my childhood. He started a small company with his older brother in Dallas in the late 1970s. Their business was selling the service of computer programmers who could program whatever you needed for your business.

For example, consider programming the fuel pumps at gas stations. They're all digital now, but in the '70s this was a brand-new thing. Dad and his brother would subcontract a programmer to perform the task and update the pump.

He didn't love the job, but that was the sacrifice he made to support his family. And like the job or not, he was *really* good with people. Dad could impress a high-level Exxon executive at a suit-and-tie dinner and also wind up becoming friends with the janitor in the bathroom of the restaurant. Everybody liked him. It didn't matter what your social status was, he could engage and find common ground with everyone.

Have you ever been to a party where the person you're talking to is glancing over your shoulder, looking toward the door to make sure someone more important than you doesn't walk in? We all know *that* guy, but that guy wasn't Dad.

He'd remind us boys that men were separated into two categories: studs and duds.

He would say, "The guys who don't care about what they wear or what others think but still set the trend anyway, the guys who don't get caught up in trash talk and bullying but still protect the vulnerable, the guys who make friends based on their heart and not their job, those are the studs. Those who aren't that? Those are the duds."

The first impression anyone got from Dad was feeling as if they'd had their hand broken. He had massive hands and the grip of a stainless-steel bench vise. Seriously, the man had the firmest handshake I've ever felt. I still laugh thinking about our childhood friends coming to the house and Dad just crushing their hands with no mercy as if they were grown men making a business deal. The tougher kids wouldn't blink an eye, but as soon as Dad turned away, they would grimace in pain and flap their hand around as if they had just pulled it off a hot stove.

I know, I know, it sounds like some kind of cruel torture, but it wasn't. I still have old friends who reach out to me and talk about that handshake.

It wasn't about Dad showing dominance over them; it was teaching them (in a memorable way) how important a man-to-man greeting was. When you're a young boy, nothing makes you feel more like a man than when another man treats you like one.

As we got older, we tried to inflict pain back onto him. You had to be quick and get that space between your thumb and pointer finger as far back into his palm as you could before his vise clamped down. I never asked him, but I can't help but wonder if I ever made him flinch a time or two. Probably not.

No one forgot meeting Chris Smith.

THE MAN

Mom and Dad had three boys. I was the oldest, Tyler came three and a half years later, and Parker, "the caboose" as they called him, came nine and a half years after Tyler. Dad knew that in order to raise three men, he needed to be *the* man.

And he was.

I'm not talking about domination, control, intimidation, fear tactics, or leverage. I'm talking about leading with wisdom for the benefit of the entire family. Yes, we were scared of him, and yes, he spanked us, but it was never out of anger or rage. He was always calm and collected, and we always deserved it. We would hear the classic line, "This will hurt me more than it'll hurt you," but judging by how much it hurt me, it must've *really* hurt him! As an adult looking back, I respect him more, not less, for his calculated discipline.

That being said, it wasn't the spankings that motivated us most in Dad's discipline; it was the heart-piercing disappointment of actually breaking his trust. Parker told me that one time he threw a party in high school, and despite all the cover-up and teenage lies, Mom and Dad still found out. Parker said that when he finally fessed up face-to-face, Dad actually cried.

I'M TALKING ABOUT LEADING WITH WISDOM FOR THE BENEFIT OF THE ENTIRE FAMILY.

I think it's important to note that Dad cried publicly at the birth of his sons and grandkids, his father's death, at the end of the movie *Sergeant York*, one time when it rained on the ranch in August during a drought, and apparently one other time—when Parker lied to him.

Parker was so crushed by Dad's tears of disappointment that

no grounding or spanking could've ever made a more lasting impression.

DIDN'T BACK DOWN

In Dallas, we didn't live in a bad part of town, but it definitely wasn't the good part either. We had our share of punks who trolled the neighborhood daily. There were so many good people who lived around us that we overlooked the bad, but you definitely couldn't completely ignore them. If we put up a basketball hoop, it would be torn down the next day. If we left a bike or lawn mower unattended, it would be stolen.

I'll say this about Dad: he never backed down from the punks. Three times I had my bicycle stolen, and all three times Dad tracked it down and stole it back.

Once he took it right out from under the unsuspecting thief while the guy was riding it. Another time he drove slowly through the back of an apartment complex, located the punks who had it, and yelled at them until they abandoned the bike and ran away on foot.

One time (and my favorite bike story), like some undercover CIA agent, he found the bike hidden in the bushes at a local park. A large group of guys was nearby. He started walking around the park whistling and calling for an imaginary dog named "Misty." He made his way close to the group, still whistling and calling, and asked the guys if they had seen his little white poodle pup. He crept closer and closer until he snatched the bike from the bushes, yelling, "This is my bike!"

The thieves ran away.

I've never really understood how he did that, but Dad was a big, intimidating man.

I can remember one evening, we were getting ready for bed, and the whole family was together. We heard some hollering in the backyard and the sound of our trash cans getting dumped over and crushed. Before I could really process what the sound was, Dad was up and in a full-pajama sprint for the back door. He ran across the yard and scaled our six-foot wooden fence, landing directly on top of the group of vandals. They bolted, and he chased them for at least a quarter mile. When he returned to the house and sat down, we noticed his foot was purple and swollen. We learned later that the bones had been shattered, but the pain had been irrelevant to him. His first priority was to protect his family.

A LIFE OF INTEGRITY

Dad didn't have hobbies or toys. There was no Harley in the garage, and he didn't take golfing trips with his buddies. He loved Mom and put everything else into raising us boys.

That's pretty rare in today's world.

He grew up loving the outdoors and did all he could on the weekends to get me and my brothers out of the concrete jungle. When the opportunity arose for him to sell his share of the computer-programming company, he never looked back. He was only forty-seven years old when he sold the business, sold the house, and bought a cattle ranch in Clifton, about two hours south of Dallas.

He ditched the suits for blue jeans and T-shirts. He traded computer consulting for farm work. Soon, everyone in the area loved my dad. He was colorfully woven into the fabric of that town.

I often find myself sitting on the back porch of his ranch. He was so much a part of that place; I can even feel him in the Hill Country wind. We still meet new people daily who have a warm remembrance about Dad—from the bank tellers to the feedstore clerks to the grocery store baggers. He made *everyone* feel like a friend, and he sincerely meant it.

Looking back, I know my dad was leading from the front. He knew that the best way to teach his boys was by living it out in front of our eyes.

Many years later, being the meticulous planner that he was, he arrived at a crossroads. With the kids out of the house, he began to think about the twilight years for him and Mom. If he didn't sell the ranch, would there be enough money for emergency medical bills? Or elderly care for them? If he died before Mom, would she be completely self-sufficient as a widow for ten years? How about twenty?

That's what led him to the unannounced job search at age sixty. Maybe he needed an extra challenge. I tend to think he was still teaching us sons about ambition. None of that mattered as much as what we found on the first line of that hidden résumé.

"Chris Smith, I am a man of integrity."

Wow. I had to ask myself, *Would I be confident enough in that definition of myself to lead off a résumé with it?*

According to him, that was his most valuable, earthly, hirable asset. He was still teaching me. I was still learning.

Although far from perfect, my dad was a living definition of that word—*integrity*. That's a crushing handshake from him that I can still feel to this day. Through the ebb and flow of life's current, it's an admirable goal to sail with the winds of integrity, even through profound grief. That was my dad's final lesson to me, and he had no idea that in five years I would cling to it with every last breath in my body.

6

RIVERS IN THE WASTELAND

There is a river whose streams make glad the city
of God, the holy habitation of the Most High. God
is in the midst of her; she shall not be moved;
God will help her when morning dawns.

Psalm 46:4–5

SMILING, ENTERTAINING, PERFORMING, pretending, distracting myself, walking back to my bus and completely breaking down. As I admitted earlier, that was the backside of 2019 for me.

Just. Keep. Moving. Forward.

I would go backstage after every show and empty my pockets: bandanna, stray guitar picks, wrinkled up condolence notes from fans, and one of River's scuffed up Lightning McQueen Hot Wheels cars.

Just. Keep. Moving. Forward.

I continually repeated it aloud to myself, thinking it was the only way. I wanted to believe it, but in truth my own common sense knew it was a lie.

There were unavoidable, looming questions on my horizon. *How much longer could I keep this music thing going?* Honestly, I didn't want to do it anymore. There were no more songs left in my heart to write. The shows were nothing more than a conscious diversion and a paycheck. I could shoulder that burden for the sake of my band's and crew's salary and health insurance, but other than that, the concerts felt empty

FOR THE FIRST TIME IN DECADES, MY GREATEST PASSION OUTSIDE OF MY FAMILY WAS PASSIONLESS.

and meaningless. For the first time in decades, my greatest passion outside of my family was passionless.

At the time, every major radio show, talk show, late show, morning show, magazine, and newspaper was still blowing up my publicist trying to get an interview from me about what had happened in my backyard on June 4. We continued to politely decline every request, but that didn't stop pop media from continuing to run their own stories based on their limited information, including police reports. Still to this day, if you type my name in a search engine, just a few results down you'll find a People.com headline, "Granger Smith's Son, River, 3, Died in a Drowning Accident at Home, Singer's Rep Confirms."

NO HIDING FROM HATERS

I couldn't protect myself from seeing the story. It was everywhere—on the radio, social media, TV, and tabloids. River's name kept surfacing, over and over and over again. Apparently it was a slow news season.

Each time something was published, a large group of the general public, outside of my fan base, would lash out at Amber and me, attacking our parenting and our character.

"He must've been drunk!"

"Someone call the cops on these idiots."

"He would be in prison for murder if he wasn't a celebrity."

"How hard is it to just watch your freakin' child?"

"Parents that leave toddlers unattended around a pool make me sick!"

"Take the other children away from them! They aren't suitable enough to parent!"

"Naming your child River and then drown him?? What kind of sick humans are they?"

I even saw where one person built an entire multipage conspiracy about how I joined a secret celebrity cult that sacrificed children to gain ultimate fame and fortune, and Lincoln would be next on my altar.

I've always considered myself an even-keeled person, but this constant onslaught was slowly eating me alive, like toxic acid. What made it worse was how media outlets were perpetuating the hatefulness, using it as clickbait for engagement.

My record label, booking agent, and publicist were fielding it all, deflecting and saving me from further pain. They are amazing people. I get choked up just thinking about what they must've gone through to help protect my family. They lashed back at journalists and cut ties with publications, all while disregarding their own business relationships to do so.

No one sacrificed more than my brother, Tyler, my manager. He and Riv were close. River loved Uncle TyTy and all the adventures they shared together.

All my kids do.

"Faster, TyTy, faster!" River was famous for shouting this to his uncle when they rode anything that had wheels.

Tyler stepped into the fire in full-on brother-protection mode not only to make sure the negative press and publishers couldn't reach me but also to try and keep me from seeing any of it. But unquestionably he did it at the cost of his own healing from the traumatic and sudden loss of his three-year-old nephew.

Nonetheless, I saw the media. Strangers flocked to my social media accounts to mount an attack in the comment section of my latest posts.

Why do we sift through hundreds of loving comments, land

on the one hateful one, and then dwell on that hate for the rest of the day? That was me.

Amber received her share of hate as well, even though she had absolutely no involvement in River's death. I warned her not to read any of the comments, but just like me, she did. Unlike me, she occasionally lashed back.

Among many other outlets, Today.com ran a story about her titled "Granger Smith's Wife Responds to 'Cruel' Comments About Son Who Died."[3] In that story they quoted Amber from an Instagram comment she wrote to several haters, saying, "I never like to give these people more attention than they deserve, but it's a reminder that we live in a dark world, where people judge one another, and say the most hurtful, cruel things. Please think before you type or speak your opinions."

Even though I preferred deleting hateful comments instead of replying to them, she was absolutely right. These stories and comments not only triggered added emotional pain for us but also confirmed the fact that social media in general provides an unhealthy platform where strangers can hide behind a keyboard and inflict what could be life-threatening damage on their target. I often read these and worried about someone who might be going through severe depression, someone who maybe didn't have the same kind of support group that I did to soften the blow. I'm confident in thinking that one hurtful comment on Facebook could lead to someone's suicide. It's *that* big of a deal, something our society desperately needs to understand.

I'm not naive enough to think that my story should be immune to this kind of offensive treatment. In fact, I'm no better than any of the other keyboard warriors.

Several years ago I remember hearing a story on the news about a two-year-old boy at a Disney World hotel who was wading at the edge of a lagoon while his parents and four-year-old sister sat close by watching fireworks. He was ankle-deep, only a foot into the water, when an alligator crept up and snatched the boy. When the horrified parents realized what had happened, they both jumped into the murky water to save him. The father tried to pry the gator's jaws open but was not successful. The gator disappeared back into the deeper water with the baby boy. Sixteen hours later, authorities found the drowned body fully intact, but it was too late.

I wish I could tell you that my first reaction to hearing this news story was genuine compassion and empathy for the family, but it wasn't. It was more along the lines of, "How could any decent parent allow this to happen?!"

I don't know that family, but somewhere in my dark days after losing Riv, they came to mind, and I wept for them and cringed at my prideful, knee-jerk judgment. The new, more informed version of myself would react with, "Oh God, my heart breaks for them. I can't even fathom how difficult this family's painstaking journey to recovery will be."

That's why the hateful comments toward my family sank so deeply into my gut. Partly because I was no different from the commenters, and partly because I agreed more with the hate speech than I did with the compassionate well-wishers. I didn't love myself for this; I hated myself for it.

The encouraging people who were posting would say, "Granger, you're an amazing dad. Don't blame yourself for this!"

I would ask myself, *Okay, what would ultimately qualify me as an amazing dad?*

Got it: keeping my kids alive.

I *was* a bad father. I *was* neglectful. I *did* deserve nothing short of prison.

I sided with the haters, and I hated them for being candid just as much as I hated myself for pretending to be repulsed by their accurate assessment of me.

INNOCENCE IS A LIE

These looping mental gymnastics gave my therapist at the Tennessee retreat a complicated challenge. The world wants to tell you that you have to forgive yourself and let go of the guilt, but a guilty man can't forgive himself when at his core he still believes he's guilty.

A GUILTY MAN CAN'T FORGIVE HIMSELF WHEN AT HIS CORE HE STILL BELIEVES HE'S GUILTY.

It's very difficult for a therapist to dismantle a core belief.

I found more commonality in my fragile mental anxiety with war vets struggling with PTSD than I did with counselors, pastors, and therapists.

Afghanistan veteran and Medal of Honor recipient Dakota Meyer and I have a paradoxical history. On June 4, 2019, just a few hours before I found River in the pool, I was a guest on his podcast along with Army Ranger sniper Nicholas Irving. Dakota and Nicholas were representing vets who struggled with the loss of life that happened around them during their time in combat and with the guilt that followed them home.

Our topic was, "What was the worst day of your life?" (I know. Ironic. That was the last interview I did as a country singer without a son in the grave. Little did I know on that podcast that my worst day would actually be later *that* day.)

At the time of the interview, my worst day was losing my dad. I can somewhat reconcile the loss of a parent, no matter how sudden or how tragic, because though Dad wasn't elderly, he had lived a vibrant and fruitful life. In addition, I had absolutely nothing to do with the cause of his passing.

Months later, I heard Dakota in an interview on Joe Rogan's podcast say that just speaking into existence his innocence regarding the loss of life couldn't wipe away his guilt for not being there to save his unit in combat. The world could tell him that he had nothing to feel guilty about, but that would only be a lie. I resonated with that and texted Dakota about it, but his answer confused me.

He said, "Granger, that was the old me. I don't think that way anymore. I need to get you on the other side of that." He continued, "I'm there finally and I'm gonna get you there. I can read the guilt you have in your words, and I can see it in your photos. I can literally feel it."

I could sense the genuine concern for me, but even a Medal of Honor recipient had no practical solution for my heaviness. Or maybe I should say I wasn't ready to hear it. What did that even mean, "I'm gonna get you there"? I was comfortless, but I hid that from the public as much as I could. I wasn't into mind games. I needed a real plan on how to continue breathing on a planet where I no longer felt at home.

LIFE IS LIKE A RIVER, AND IT CONTINUES TO MOVE FORWARD, BUT I SURE COULDN'T.

During this time, I asked many other war-tortured veterans similar questions about how to continue forward with PTSD. Former Navy SEAL Marcus Luttrell graciously spoke with me early on after our traumatic experience. He still checks in with me every few months. The resounding answer from those guys was something like this: "Losing a friend in battle, holding him in your arms knowing maybe you could have done more to save him, is a reality that is nearly impossible to live with. But losing a son like you did, I don't have an answer for that. I just can't imagine."

Life is like a river, and it continues to move forward, but I sure couldn't.

THE NUMBING (DE)VICE

Lacking a real answer to my struggle, I continued to stack on the music and life distractions. My touring routine looked like this: Hide all morning until sound check. Get a quick workout at the gym to sweat out some anxiety. No interviews. No meet and greets. Begrudgingly carve through a performance with fake smiles and forgotten lyrics. Retreat back to the bus. I would shower, brush my teeth, and crawl into my twin-size bed in Wildflower's back bedroom. I was exhausted, but sleep wouldn't come. The truth is, I was terrified to close my eyes because that was a surefire way to initiate the slideshow. I didn't have the attention span to read a book, didn't have the courage to journal, and it was too late at night to FaceTime Amber and the kids back in Texas.

I certainly couldn't leave that little room. Outside, a bunch of well-meaning band and crew members were sipping whiskey and incessantly asking me whether "everything was all right."

It wasn't.

I made a new rule of the road: don't ask me that question anymore.

I tried to lose myself in Netflix and YouTube, but there seemed to be a drowning reference in every film—like a lion lying in wait to devour me.

The best alternative I had was simply lying there staring at the lights on the ceiling.

One day some friends approached me.

"Looks like you haven't slept in a while, huh?" They were concerned about my appearance.

"Ever thought about weed? Ya know, it's becoming more and more accepted in the medical community to help with physical pain and insomnia."

No. I hadn't thought about that, but at least it was a practical, applicable idea. I rattled it around for a bit in my skeptical brain. Numbing with a buzz? I barely even drank alcohol in the few years prior because it just slowed me down in a schedule that needed to move fast. Plus, weed was for lazy people, right? That was my limited perception of it. I made my mental calculations. At that point I really didn't care anymore. This was a dire circumstance.

On our next trip to Denver, Colorado, I set out for a dispensary to buy some marijuana.

The place was like a candy store that offered every consumable option and flavor. My first purchase of THC came in small 5 mg capsules that you pour onto food. My second purchase was vaping oil. The capsules with food didn't do much for me, but I felt the oil instantly.

After the show I took a shower, brushed my teeth, turned off the lights, and crawled into bed. I powered on the newly charged battery in the little vape pen and gave it a few seconds to heat up on the lowest setting. I put it to my lips, squeezed the button down, inhaled, and waited. Within seconds the numbing sensation came over me like a warm blanket.

I took another drag of the pen and set it down on the nightstand.

From under the covers I gazed up at the ceiling lights. I felt like I was melting deeper into the mattress, minute by minute. More relaxed, and then even more. My anxious thoughts seemed to evaporate into nothingness. I had nowhere to be, nothing to do, and nothing on my mind.

Those ceiling lights had never seemed interesting before, but suddenly it seemed I could watch them for hours, as if they were the most captivating thing on the planet. *How does electricity work? Where does it come from? Whoa.* What an incredible phenomenon those lights were! I broke into a grin. I wanted to get up and tell someone else about this modern marvel, but I was way too comfortable to move.

Eight hours later I opened my eyes, fully rested after an entire night's sleep. Wow! I actually slept uninterrupted for the first time in months. No slideshow and no sad emotions. Honestly, there were no emotions of *any* kind that night.

I now had a solid plan. Stay close to the pen, then surrender to it when the slideshow became unbearable. I plugged it back in to charge the battery for another night.

This is how I coped with the tour-life nights, and to my best understanding at the time, this was the only way to find rest for the weary. But it was only temporary.

It didn't take long before I stressed about the nightmares happening off tour as well, so I bought a second emergency pen and more oil to use at home. I used that on nights when I felt anxious in my own bed, but it quickly became an every-night preventative measure just in case a panic attack ensued. If I was lucky enough to fall asleep without a slideshow viewing, that didn't guarantee that it wouldn't wake me up a few hours later with a vengeance. So I would take a shower, brush my teeth, put on my pj's, and hit the pen.

Amber would walk into a white vape cloud in our bathroom and chuckle, "Okay, Snoop Dogg, time for bed." She never questioned my intentions. If anyone truly understood my desperately urgent grasp for survival, it was her. When you're drowning in a river, you'll do just about anything to find the air.

THE BURNING HOUSE

I know the exact moment when I realized that this was a big problem.

One night I was camping with our kids at our company headquarters that we call the Yee Yee Farm. We set up a tent, made a campfire, cooked dinner, and made s'mores over the open flames. It was a beautiful evening with smiles and hot grilled cheese sandwiches. About 9:00 p.m., when both London and Lincoln were sound asleep in their sleeping bags next to me, I lay between them staring up through the tent screen at the Texas stars, listening over the crackles of the dying campfire to a pack of coyotes yelping in the distance.

Like a crafty thief of peace, it came upon me.

The slideshow.

River was facedown in the pool again.

Do these kids realize that you killed their little brother?

The guilt.

And then, as always, the panic.

Tears burst into my eyes, and my throbbing heart rushed into my throat. *Oh no. I forgot my weed pen.* In terror-stricken alarm I thought about Wildflower—she was parked only three hundred yards away in our bus barn at the office. My touring pen was tucked away in her bedroom drawer. I flung open the sleeping bag and bounced off, sprinting through the night pasture, barefoot and knee-deep in bluestem grass. I got to the bus, warmed up the pen, took a long drag, and shoved it into my pocket for insurance.

I took off running back toward the tent, guided by the last few flames of the fire in the dark night, and by the time I got there and zipped the sleeping bag back around my body, I felt the warm, sedative medicine doing its work.

I was appalled at my weakness. I really was a terrible father. How long would I need this vice?

A few more months?

A few more years?

The rest of my life?

One thing became clear that night: the weed oil wasn't healing me from any pain; it was simply numbing it. It was a way of kicking the can farther and farther down the road, but I would eventually have to deal with it.

I was trapped in a burning house, sitting on the living room floor, and building a little brick wall around me to numb the sting from the heat. At some point I was going to need to stand up, face the flame, and run directly toward it to find the exit. Yes, I might get burned (maybe badly), but when you're engulfed in flames, moving toward them is the only way out.

WHEN YOU'RE ENGULFED IN FLAMES, MOVING TOWARD THEM IS THE ONLY WAY OUT.

Maybe this is what Dakota Meyer and Marcus Luttrell were trying to show me.

Looking back now, I know that true healing is connected with our willingness to run through the pain, not away from it. But I didn't know that yet, much less know what it meant.

I was battling to somehow get upstream. I tried to slow down the current, but it wasn't working. I simply didn't know any other way to navigate the river through the wasteland.

ME AND DAD. I STILL LEARN FROM HIM EVEN AFTER HE'S GONE.

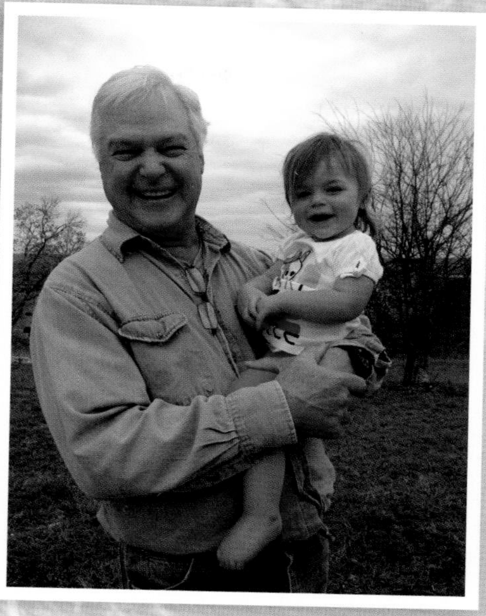

ONE OF THE FEW PICTURES OF LONDON WITH DAD. SHE WAS TWO AND HALF YEARS OLD WHEN HE PASSED IN 2014.

RIVER CUDDLED IN MY LAP BEFORE WE FILMED THE "HAPPENS LIKE THAT" MUSIC VIDEO. HE LOVED TO HEAR ME PLAY AND SING!

LONDON AND RIVER PICKING FLOWERS FOR MAMA.

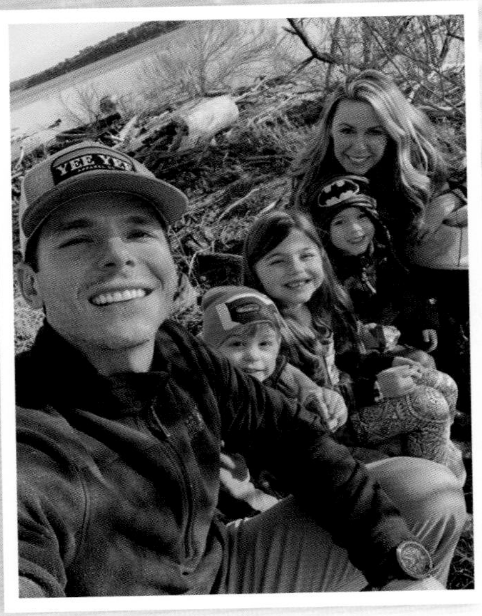

LOTS OF SMILES ON A FAMILY HIKING TRIP IN EARLY 2019.

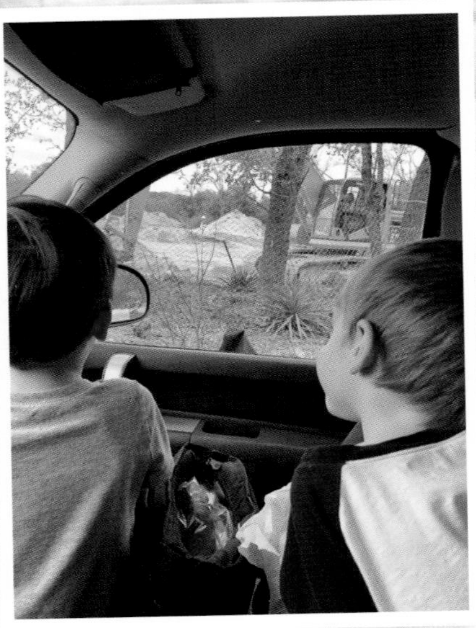

LINCOLN AND RIVER WATCHING AN EXCAVATOR ON THE SIDE OF THE ROAD. THAT WAS RIVER'S FAVORITE TRACTOR.

LINCOLN AND RIVER WERE BEST BUDS. THIS WAS ABOUT TWO MONTHS BEFORE WE LOST HIM.

RIVER LOVED HIS TOY TRACTOR WITH A SUPERSIZED BATTERY!

RIVER, LINCOLN, AND LONDON. I TOOK THIS PIC OF THEM CHEESIN'.

WE LOVED RIDING AROUND THE WOODS ON WHAT WE THOUGHT WAS OUR FOREVER HOME PROPERTY.

ME, RIVER, AND HIS WILD RED HAIR.

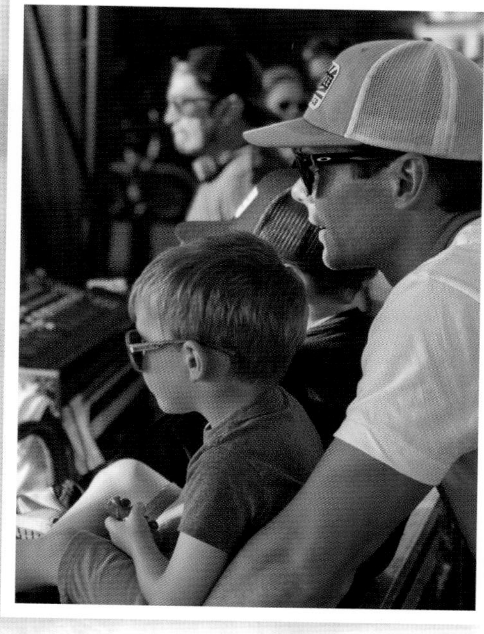

RIVER WATCHING THE OPENING BAND WITH ME BEFORE MY CONCERT. WE LOST HIM THAT NEXT WEEK.

THE NURSES PUT RIVER'S FAVORITE TOY IN HIS HAND. AMBER AND I TOOK THIS PICTURE MOMENTS BEFORE THEY WHEELED HIM AWAY.

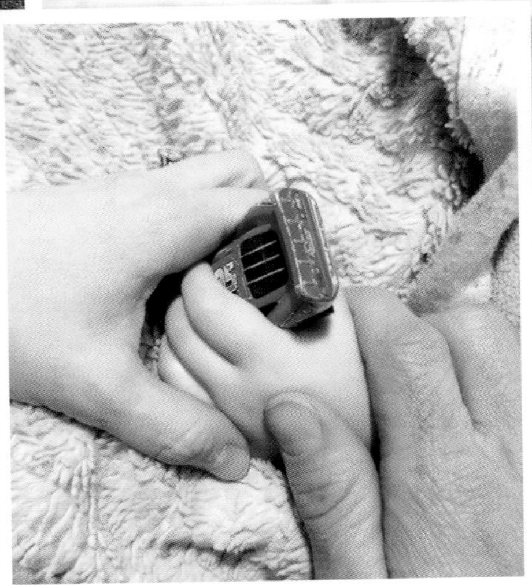

RIVER'S FORGOTTEN TOYS IN THE BACKYARD. I TOOK THIS PICTURE KNOWING THAT HE WAS THE LAST ONE TO HAVE TOUCHED THEM.

THE PRE-SHOW BACKSTAGE MOMENTS AFTER WE LOST RIV WERE BRUTAL.

I THOUGHT GOING BACK ON THE ROAD WOULD HELP—BUT I WAS JUST GOING THROUGH THE MOTIONS AND PROLONGING MY HEALING.

THE FAMILY OF FOUR. AMBER AND I WERE FRESH OUT OF THERAPY IN NOVEMBER 2019. PUSHING FORWARD.

AMBER TRAVELED WITH ME AS MUCH AS POSSIBLE. THIS WAS PRE-SHOW VALENTINE'S DAY 2020.

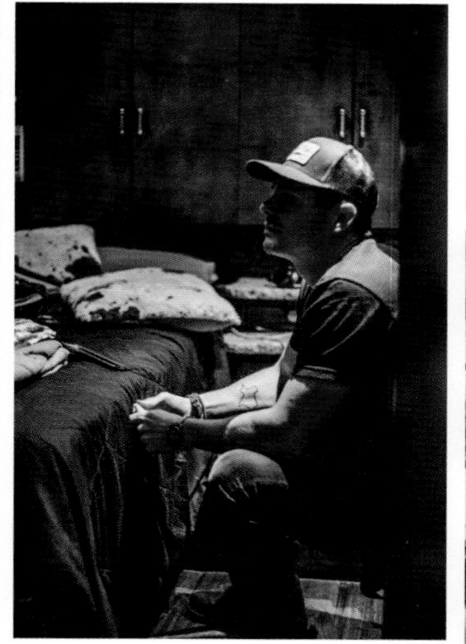

MY LITTLE ROOM IN THE BACK OF MY BUS, WILDFLOWER.

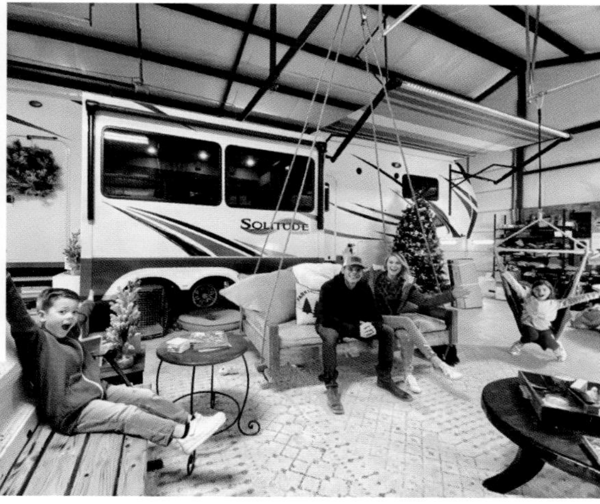

LIFE IN THE RV PARKED IN THE BARN! THE CHRISTMAS TREE LOOKED GREAT IN THERE.

THE *TODAY* SHOW SET UP IN OUR LIVING ROOM OF OUR "IN BETWEEN HOME" TO TALK TO US FOR THE FIRST TIME PUBLICLY ABOUT LOSING RIV. IT WAS MARCH 2020.

I SNAPPED THIS PIC OF THE FAMILY CHECKING OUT THE NEW LITTLE FARM FOR THE FIRST TIME. THEY ARE STANDING WHERE OUR HOUSE NOW SITS.

WHILE WE WERE BUILDING A HOUSE ON OUR NEW LAND, AN ICE STORM DEVASTATED MANY OF OUR OLD TREES. THAT TAUGHT ME A BIG LESSON ON LOVING THINGS OF THIS WORLD.

WE'RE PREGNANT! THIS WAS OUR BABY MAVERICK ANNOUNCEMENT.

MY FIRST TIME PREACHING AT A CHURCH WAS IN AUGUST OF 2021. THE STAGE WASN'T NEW FOR ME, BUT MY MESSAGE WAS.

THE BIBLE THAT TRANSFORMED MY LIFE, WHICH I READ SO OFTEN SITTING IN THAT CHAIR IN THE BARN AFTER MY REBIRTH.

EARLY MORNING COFFEE AND BIBLE STUDY IN THE BARN. I BEGAN A ROUTINE BACK THEN THAT I STILL DO TODAY. I HAVEN'T SKIPPED A SINGLE MORNING SINCE 2020.

AMBER MEETS MAVERICK FOR THE FIRST TIME.

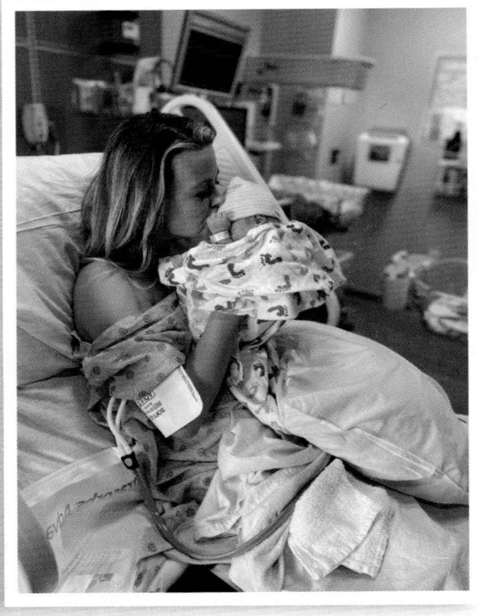

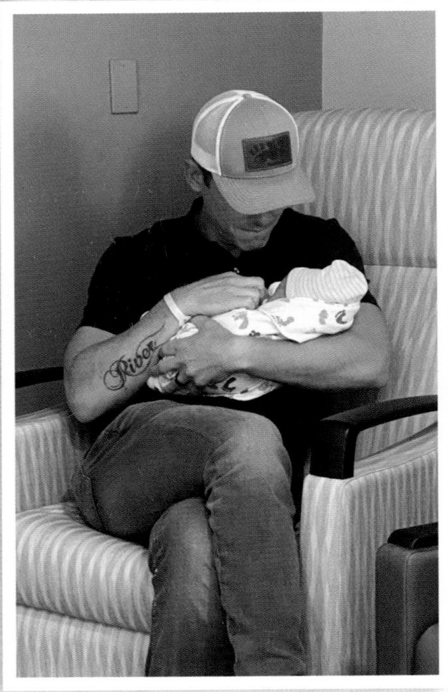

THERE WERE SOME PRETTY INTENSE EMOTIONS HOLDING MAV ON HIS BIRTHDAY. RIVER TATTOO ON MY ARM.

BABY MAV GETTING ALL THE ATTENTION IN THE HOUSE.

LONDON AND LINCOLN ARE CAPTIVATED BY THEIR LITTLE BROTHER MAV.

7

THE DARK NIGHT OF THE SOUL

The earth was without form and void, and darkness
was over the face of the deep. And the Spirit of
God was hovering over the face of the waters.

Genesis 1:2

AT THE END OF NOVEMBER 2019, my life's river had widened a bit to allow for smoother sailing. The hull of my boat was still damaged and slowly taking on water, but I had some tools to help keep it bailed out and keep me from drowning. Yet it was a grim miscalculation to think that calm waters are a result of our oars and paddle technique. In reality they are dictated by the Source of the river. To a small extent we can balance ourselves with effort and persistence, but once the river reaches a certain level of turbulence, even the strongest, most-skilled sailors will capsize.

The oars in my boat were my wooden weapons. I had my self-help repertoire packed with a thousand feel-good, one-liner quotes about how the power was within me for living my best life and how to take full responsibility for my own destiny. I had my ten-minute morning meditations and kale-blended protein shakes. I was avoiding processed foods that could cloud my thinking, especially while struggling with depression. I was exercising and drinking lots of water. I had ingrained the mantras of Tony Robbins's deep, raspy voice on YouTube saying things like, "Your past doesn't equal your future." I had my little one-page Christian devotionals with the cute, feel-good, "God loves me" Bible verses. I had coping skills and pragmatic practices I had learned from a highly esteemed therapy treatment center, and I had the most immediately effective wooden stick, the weed pen.

I also had plenty of oil on standby.

If I diligently kept up this regimen, I believed that, over time, my days would get easier and easier until my new normal would become manageable. Then ultimately, after a lot of hard work, I could experience true happiness again.

Sure, I could never move on from the loss of my son, but I could still move forward by my own power and embrace his memory as a reminder to live life the way he would've wanted me to.

All of that sounds so beautiful.

It sounds doable.

But that's not what happened.

This story isn't finished yet.

All those things served a purpose in navigating the river in what now was just a raft, but when I drifted into a waterfall, they became useless oars in a capsizing boat.

THE TEMPORARY VICTORY

The waters were relatively calm going into our first River-less Thanksgiving.

It had been nearly five months since our lives had changed. My mom hosted the holiday at her house at the ranch, which provided us with a well-received change of scenery. Amber and I were just a few days removed from our therapy retreat. I fasted for twenty-four hours before that meal to make sure that I had a clear mind and body to be better equipped to live presently and not dwell on the past. (I had learned that constructive technique before we shared the first Thanksgiving meal after Dad passed.)

We smiled, we cried, we told stories, and we ate turkey and dressing. I survived it.

The first week of December, we bused off for a rigorous twenty-two-day, sold-out tour on the West Coast. A jam-packed holiday season tour schedule had been booked by design to offer the continued work distraction that I craved. Night after night I chiseled through the concerts and flew home for the occasional days off. I practiced my brainspotting skills, forced myself to double down on the self-help books, and slept by means of the weed pen. I had more of a controlled grip on my anxiety during these touring days. During some of the shows, while playing some of the songs, I might've even lost myself in the music and enjoyed the moment again. It was nice.

Nearing the end of the tour, on December 19, we arrived in Boise, Idaho, where we parked the buses for three days. We were scheduled for two days of back-to-back shows plus a third day off before we traveled again to Salt Lake City.

On day two, with plenty of time to kill, my guitar player, John Marlin (I call him Fish), and I decided to go snow skiing at the nearby Bogus Basin Resort. We rented a car, rented some skis, and ventured up the mountain. After only a few runs down the hill, Fish and I got separated. When I finally found him, he had taken a pretty nasty spill and was laid out with a painful broken collar bone. I took him to the ER where the X-ray showed just how bad the break was. The good news was we weren't traveling for the next two days, but the bad news was he needed immediate surgery. I reluctantly left him there in the hospital and went on to a passionate Boise crowd to play the concert minus one guitar player.

Although it was an extremely painful accident for Fish, this change of protocol gave me a more deliberate distraction. It provided a new point of focus to pour my concentration into and a chance to really nail this concert shorthanded.

Sometimes for me, after playing too many concerts in a row with the same songs to similar-looking crowds, I have a tendency to start daydreaming on stage and lose my firm grip on the present moment. I had been working on this for years in an effort to really soak up the moments—while I'm in my prime and I still have the chance. I wasn't getting any younger, and I knew that one day I would walk off the stage after the last best concert of my life and not even realize it at the time. It's kind of like that story I've heard that says at some point in your childhood, you and your friends went outside to play together for the last time, and none of you knew it. I felt that.

Additionally, in my unstable, anxious condition after losing Riv, daydreaming was a doorway to sadness, so an excuse to really concentrate on plugging the holes from the missing guitar parts was a welcome diversion.

From my perspective the show wasn't perfect, but we filled the missing pieces with color and energy. The crowd was forgiving, loud, and wildly passionate. I actually had a really good time. After the show we celebrated the victory with a round of whiskey shots for the band and crew.

One for Fish's speedy recovery!

One for us! And then . . . another one for us!

We had earned it. I definitely felt like I had earned it. It had been a long time since I had sipped some whiskey in celebration with my boys.

MY DARKEST NIGHT

That show was a milestone for me. After nearly seven months of struggle, heartache, and anxiety, all while exhaustingly hiding my pain, that night I didn't want to retreat to Wildflower. Some of the guys found a small, inconspicuous bar directly across the street from where our buses were parked and invited the rest of us to join for a nightcap or two. I didn't hesitate.

Yes!

I was officially ready to get my life back—or at least I was finally ready to regain some sense of normalcy again—and I couldn't think of a better time and place than right there with my road brothers who had carried me on tour through a terribly dark season. They are great guys. When I was alone, they gave me companionship. When I forgot the words to my songs, they encouraged me. When I didn't want to show up at all, they supported me and validated all of it.

We were the only ones in the little bar that night. We sat on stools and told old stories, some of which we'd heard a hundred times and others old memories that we'd almost forgotten about.

We laughed about the days when we crammed into a van; shared run-down, roach-infested motel rooms; and played rock-paper-scissors to decide who would sleep on the mattresses and who would sleep on the box springs that we pulled off to make more beds.

We reminisced about our first vintage tour bus that seeped diesel fumes between the couch cushions and how we were amazed that we even woke up each morning after that much carbon monoxide poisoning. We talked about old band members who had come and gone in years past, and several times I retold the story about Fish wrapped up tightly lying on the ski patrol sled—a "fish taco." We had some good laughs that night as the bartender refilled our whiskey glasses again and again.

Eventually, as it got later and later, I said my farewells and pushed back from the bar.

"Hey, it was really good to see you like this, boss. I'm really happy you came out with us tonight."

"Me too, buddy. I love you guys," I answered back to our monitor engineer, Will.

As I walked out onto the sidewalk, the frigid Idaho air took my breath away.

It was freezing.

I walked quickly across the street to Wildflower and fumbled with the door handle. *What was the code to the keypad lock again?* My vision was blurry, and I couldn't make out the numbers that I'd typed a thousand times before.

Five . . . three . . . wait, is it two or . . . dang it. I was pretty drunk. The world was spinning around me.

Concentrate! I dug at myself.

Finally, I got it unlocked and stumbled onto the bus.

I was dizzy as I bounced my shoulders off bunks and bus walls, trampling down the hallway to the back room, my lonely cave of solitude.

THE CONCERT MIGHT'VE FELT NORMAL, BUT THAT BACK ROOM REMINDED ME THAT MY LIFE STILL WASN'T.

The concert might've felt normal, but that back room reminded me that my life still wasn't. Self-help books scattered on the bed, motivational quotes on the dry-erase board, my weed pen on the charger—these were all reminders of a desperate man's continued struggle to survive.

I picked up the weed pen. "Better take a good drag of this to protect myself from the slideshow tonight," I said.

Wait . . .

The slideshow.

I hadn't thought about that all night long. A terrifying realization began to roll up from my belly and into my neck. This was the first time I'd been drunk since . . .

My heart rate increased.

The room was now spinning faster.

How could I be so stupid? Would the buzz hinder my ability to fight off the visions? Would the whiskey distort any progress I'd made with all my therapy?

Oh no.

I was relapsing. I grabbed the pen and inhaled as though my life depended on it.

And then it happened. The slideshow burst into my mind, vivid and crystal clear.

River is facedown in the pool.

I crash into the water.

I turn him over. His face is blue, eyes wide open and rolled back into his forehead, limbs dangling like a rag doll.

I clenched my face. *No. No. No. No.* The weed wasn't working. *Nothing* was working! Big tears exploded down my cheeks and puddled onto the bus floor.

"Oh, Riv. I'm so sorry. I failed you. I failed you, buddy. You trusted me, your daddy, and I failed you!"

I began to sob uncontrollably. I couldn't breathe. I couldn't move. I couldn't see anything other than River's lifeless face: so innocent, so vulnerable, and now just a ghost of a life seemingly wasted.

My fragile boat hurtled off the edge of the waterfall and into the deep abyss below. Under the depths at the rocky river bottom, with the impossible weight of surging water plummeting on top of me, I was entombed. When a desperate man is drowning, he'll do whatever it takes to find the air. He'll do whatever it takes to end the torment that's suffocating him.

Even in my utter insanity, I knew where the air was. With trembling hands I fumbled through the drawer in my closet and found it.

My 9 mm Glock. The slideshow continued, louder and even more vivid.

I'm doing CPR next to the pool, counting *one*, *two*, *three*, *four*, pumping the chest again.

Not too hard! You might break his tiny chest cavity. Or is it too late to worry about that now?

I blow into his lungs again. Amber runs toward me from the house in her bathrobe. Her face is horror-stricken. I have killed her perfect baby boy.

How could she ever forgive me for this?

She won't.

I yanked back the slide and a 9 mm bullet tumbled into the chamber. Glocks don't have a safety. I wrapped my finger around the trigger as I slid the cold barrel into my mouth. I knew that pistol very well and all of its predictabilities. I've put at least a thousand rounds through it, and even in my inebriated state, as I applied pressure on the double trigger with my index finger, I knew exactly where the point of no return would be. I gradually squeezed tighter until I recognized the spot.

There it is.

I held the pressure there without moving or adding any more to it. Tears dripped from my chin and splashed off the steel of the Glock and onto my hand. I continued the hold. If the pistol didn't work, I had a sharp knife. I could slide that into the soft part of my throat and accomplish the same end goal. None of it would hurt worse than the pain I was feeling now.

The room whirled around me, and so did my mind. I squinted my eyes shut.

You're a coward!

I recognized my own conscience screaming at me.

You're such a coward, a no-good dad who failed at the one job expected of a father, and now you're too weak to deal with your own guilt!

I was already a murderer. This would serve me well. My final contribution to the world would be to justly carry out my own capital punishment. Seconds ticked by slower than minutes.

I knew the voice of my own thoughts, but right then I noticed an unfamiliar one. It was in my head like a faint whisper that was warm, calm, and inviting, yet confident and clear.

The voice in my mind spoke.

"*It's okay . . . it's okay. You tried so hard. It's finally time to let go. This is where you'll find peace. This is the only way. All of your pain will go away . . . just squeeze.*"

Fear gripped me.

Who in the world was feeding me this? It was in my mind, but it wasn't my thought. Someone or some*thing* was with me.

Or *in* me.

My eyes opened. I was suddenly terrified of something far worse than my own guilt. There was an intruder in my presence. I was paralyzed by this new realization—I wasn't alone in the room that night. I had been hunted, ambushed, flanked, surrounded, and put under attack by an enemy far beyond my ability to defeat.

I knew it all at once.

Unconsciously, my hand ripped the pistol out of my mouth, and my voice cried out in desperation:

"My God, my Jesus! Save me! Save me, Jesus!"

The echo of my own scream bounced off the walls of the bus, and the slideshow abruptly snapped to black. The room stopped spinning. The Glock slid off my tear-soaked hand and onto the bed. Weeping bitterly, I fell to the floor.

My mind raced and shifted. I thought about two people—London and Lincoln. I saw their faces, beautiful and innocent. I repeated the plea for help again, this time in more of a choked whisper, "My God, my Jesus! Save me! Save me, Jesus!"

My heart was sick. My stomach was sick. I was so humiliated

about what I had done, or what I had almost done, or even worse, what something else was convincing me to do. I didn't know a lot about this sort of thing, but I knew enough to identify it and call it by name. This was spiritual warfare.

How long was I held captive by this dark enemy? How long did I hold the door open for him to mock me, test me, toy with me in my utter weakness without offering any kind of formidable resistance or shield? My wooden weapons were useless in this battle. That thought made me shudder until my next thought.

HOW LONG WAS I HELD CAPTIVE BY THIS DARK ENEMY?

If this enemy was so impenetrable, so invisible, so damaging to me, how much more infinitely powerful was the One I had called on to save me? That was beyond my ability to understand.

I lay there, still dressed in my show clothes, and did not reach for the weed pen. Instead, I repeated over and over, "Jesus, save me. Please, save me."

My breathing slowed, my heartbeat stabilized, my tears dried, and I fell asleep on the cold floor.

If this story sounds unbelievable, I understand. For the most part, I'm a logical person and could barely comprehend any of it myself. But if you're questioning my sanity now, that wasn't the last time I felt a spirit that was not my own. This part of my story was only just beginning.

8

REBIRTH

Whoever drinks of the water that I will give him will never be thirsty again. The water that I will give him will become in him a spring of water welling up to eternal life.

John 4:14

I DIDN'T TELL ANYONE ABOUT my dark night of the soul in Boise, not even Amber. In fact, it was still a secret three and a half years later when I began to put together the outline for this book. On the day I was scheduled to turn in the outline to my agency for them to begin pitching this book idea to publishers, I decided that I had waited long enough, and I called her.

Me: I need to tell you something extremely vulnerable about this book that soon the entire world will know.

Amber: Okay, what is it?

I told her the whole story: the concert in Boise, the celebration with the band, my weakness in dealing with the unbearable slideshow, the gun, the voice of the Liar, the ambush, my surrender to Jesus.

We cried together on the phone, and she expressed how sorry she was that I had had to go through that all alone and carry it with me for so long. She suggested that I call my brothers and my mom to tell them before they heard or read about it secondhand, so I made those difficult phone calls soon after.

How would you feel about sharing your most vulnerable, most humiliating secret with millions of strangers on a public platform? I certainly didn't love the idea myself and still don't. It's hard. The only reason I am sharing the details of my dark night now is that I believe my being open and vulnerable will resonate with someone who needs to hear there is hope and a way out.

Maybe you are that person, and if you are, please keep reading. The dark night in Boise was the catalyst to what happened next, and what happened next is the part that is the most critical for you to know.

It took dying to who I was and what I had become at the rock bottom of that river to realize that nothing in my own power could change the course of my stream.

I couldn't control it.

I couldn't change it.

I couldn't manipulate it.

I couldn't survive it.

But most reassuringly, I didn't have to. All I had to do was connect with the Source of it and surrender to it.

When I finally did that, I realized my story was only just beginning.

THE DOG-TAG CHRISTIAN

The morning after the dark night, I was still on the floor, fully dressed from T-shirt to boots. It was very rare in my life that I actually got drunk enough to pass out. I had been sick a few times before the sun came up, so I was lying close to the toilet in the back of Wildflower. I love that bus. If she could talk, she'd have many stories to tell, some of which aren't worth repeating. I've ridden her through nearly every town large and small in forty-eight states, all the provinces in Canada, beaches, deserts, prairies, forests, mountain passes, and even New York City, all many times over. She's been to state fairs, county fairs, country fairs, and countless bars and theaters that were unfair. She's seen music video sets, late-night and morning-show sets, movie sets, and sunsets. Through her windshield I've chased tornadoes, volcanoes, forest fires, blizzards, full moons, and sunrises that took my breath away. I've left her at truck stops, and she's left me at airports. She's watched my kids come and go, and one that never returned. We've both seen each other broken down more times than I can count, but we've always ended up back home safe together. Out of all our wild adventures, however, this was the only time I'd ever slept on her floor.

I got up, took a shower, and made some coffee, still decompressing after my vivid recounting of the events the night before. I didn't speak to anyone about it. I was struggling to find the missing puzzle pieces. What had happened? Whose was that voice in my head that told me, *It's finally time to let go*? Some cartoon, red-skinned, horn-headed devil on my shoulder? Surely that was my own alcohol-fueled insanity. Why did I call to Jesus, and how did that demolish the slideshow?

I had so many questions but not many answers.

Jesus was not a new name for me. At the time I was a Dog-Tag Christian, at least that's the phrase I use now. It comes from a practice during World War II where the military stamped the name of the soldier's religion on their dog tags so that if they died, people would know what kind of holy man should speak at the funeral.

I grew up in a Christian home, with a mother who read the entire New Testament to me as an infant while I nursed. I went to Sunday school every week and learned about Adam and Eve, Noah's ark, and Moses parting the Red Sea. I learned that Jesus was born in a manger, healed the sick, forgave sins, died on a cross, and rose from the dead, announcing that all who believed in Him would have eternal life. When I was twelve years old, I confessed my belief in all this and was baptized in a Methodist confirmation class. I had a head knowledge of fundamental Christian doctrine. I often prayed before meals and ended the prayer with "In Jesus' name, amen."

In high school, I attended Fellowship of Christian Athletes, youth groups, and church camps. On rare occasions, I would pick up a Bible and find some of the red-letter words but not really understand what they meant in context with the black words. That didn't concern me, because they sounded nice. There was no need to understand something that wasn't meant to be understood, right? Dad told me that the most important thing was accepting Jesus as my Lord and Savior, and I *had* checked off that box when I was twelve. Truthfully, though, it did feel kind of silly to need a "savior" when I really didn't have anything to be saved from. The Christian religion in my life had become more of a cultural heritage, and I defended it that way. But when times got tough, by no means did I consider it a life raft. Yes, I was a Dog-Tag Christian.

By the time I went to college at Texas A&M, going to church was very rare for me. I went maybe once or twice a year, but only with friends if they invited me. It's not that I disliked it, but it was kind of boring, and I was hungry, and the Cowboys were playing football, and the church was full of smiley people who were probably judging me for my torn blue jeans.

When Amber and I got married, we didn't go to church together, even though when we started having babies I felt compelled to take them just so they could grow up with Christianity the way I did. That seemed like the right thing to do, but I still didn't go to church with them. How could I? On Sundays, I was either flying home during the service times or so tired from a late Saturday night concert that the last thing I wanted to do was get dressed and go back into a crowd of people singing songs. Feeling convicted, Amber began getting more involved in women's groups at a local church and started taking the kids on Sundays without me. I was at least reading my daily devotionals. It was a weak effort, but it made me feel like I was still casting a vote on the Christian ballot.

BROKEN PARACHUTE

Before my dark night in Boise, I wasn't so sure that my Dog-Tag Christian label was still worth anything. If you were to ask me then on a scale of one to ten how sure I was about going to heaven, I'd probably say a ten. That was my ego talking based solely on the way I was raised and my proud American Christian heritage, which boasts that once you recite a prayer or raise a hand in church accepting Jesus into your heart as your Lord and Savior, your eternal destiny in heaven is secure. That prayer could be a genuine response to authentic faith, but it could also be dangerous because it can create false assurance. Looking back now, that was a broken parachute. How do I know this? Because besides reciting a prayer and understanding the fundamental Christian ideals, my life had no evidence of a repentant, regenerative heart that was fully chasing after Jesus. Sometimes we need a new perspective and a new parachute.

SOMETIMES WE NEED A NEW PERSPECTIVE AND A NEW PARACHUTE.

I want to pause here and tell you that I've labored in writing this section of the book for two reasons:

1. I don't want to downplay the work of my faithful parents in instilling Jesus into my life or to undermine the healthy seeds planted within me at an early age by so many.
2. I also want to balance that with a legitimate fear that some readers might be currently living a similar lifestyle as I was. The common Dog-Tag Christian should be very

> worried if they grew up in church, recited a typical salvation prayer at the altar, but show no proof of regeneration in their life. Let me flip the mirror around on myself and say this as bluntly as I can: if I had died that night in Boise, I wouldn't have made it to heaven. Thankfully, God's story for my life wasn't in its final chapter yet.

However, all of this was not obvious to me at the time. I didn't look for a new parachute; instead, I set out to repair the broken one. I could carve out a little space in my schedule to learn more about Jesus. After all, He was a powerful weapon against bad visions and spiritual warfare. I could use Him.

I needed a preacher.

That was my first idea, but I didn't know of any except one. It was a name I'd heard before: the Reverend Billy Graham. What could the late, great Billy Graham teach me? I decided that I would forgo the self-help audiobooks in my truck and replace that time with Rev. Graham sermons on YouTube. Sometimes they were in black and white, and he was young and dark-headed. In more recent videos he was older with silver hair. For most of the videos he was middle-aged, standing in any one of the massive stadiums around the world where he preached to a crowd of fifty thousand or more. I probably listened to more than one hundred sermons during those next couple of months. From my Dog-Tag Christian lens, none of this was new, earth-shattering information, but I figured it was good for parachute repairing. They were comfortably predictable in content that went something like this:

> We are all sinners in need of a savior. God came to earth in the person of Jesus to redeem and gather His people. He healed the sick, cast out demons, and taught about the kingdom of heaven. Labeled a blasphemous heretic by religious leaders, He

> was crucified on a cross but rose from the dead three days later at a real time in recorded history, in a real location. He revealed Himself to hundreds of real eyewitnesses, claiming that anyone who believed in Him would have peace, rest, and, most importantly, eternal life in a place where all tears would be wiped away, forever.

At this point, Billy would glue the narrative together with a relevant pop-culture reference using a Beatles song lyric or a popular Hollywood film. Then he would continue, and I would listen:

> Many of these eyewitness believers fled the persecution in Jerusalem to spread this good news to others around the world. They wrote down the stories of Jesus, and most of them were killed for it. Unexplainably, although separated by decades of time and continents of distance, all the written stories were virtually the same. Nearly six thousand of these fragmented documents are surviving today, with still more and more copies currently being discovered. That is much more than any other ancient writing in human history. If it all were a lie, they wouldn't have died for it. If they were all crazy, it would be impossible to keep their stories straight. If anyone tried to change the stories later, they never would've been able to sensibly manage all the lost copies. That leaves only one other option—it was true.

Billy Graham ended every message with the same call to action: Jesus is the only way to heaven. Repent and turn from your old self. Confess with your mouth that Jesus is Lord and believe in your heart that God raised Him from the dead, and you will be saved. In each video, thousands of people would make their way down from the bleachers and join Billy in his prayer.

You can imagine how silly I must have looked, driving around in my pickup truck, windows down on a backroad, headed to the farm listening to these Rev. Graham sermons that were older than I was.

I didn't care what anyone thought.

I liked them.

A new passion was growing within me that I didn't quite understand yet. My eyes were slowly opening.

WAVES IN A RIVER

I watched so many archived Billy Graham videos that, regardless of what decade it was filmed or where he was preaching, I pretty much knew exactly what he was going to say and how he was going to land his main point. You've probably learned by now that I'm kind of obsessive like that, especially once I get passionate about something.

I still hadn't given up on my old routine—ten minutes of morning meditation with Ten Percent Happier, one page of a Christian devotional, journaling, exercising, reading self-help books, and of course, sleeping with the weed pen. I now had my doubts about the effectiveness of any of it, but I was too indoctrinated in the self-help religion to quit. My only deviation from the original plan was trading the truck-time audiobooks for Billy Graham.

I was extremely cautious, didn't go anywhere near alcohol, and was still trying to process the dark night in Boise, thinking maybe I had learned my lesson and regained control of my boat.

Amber and I still had some heart-wrenching moments, but

touring is slow in January and February, so we were together to serve each other as a support system.

When grieving, two people are rarely on the same grief schedule. Some days one person is really struggling and the other is not, while other days the roles unpredictably reverse. It is such a great thing to be able to lean on each other when one is weaker and the other is stronger. It was also helpful that Amber and I were both heavily distracted by a new, developing situation that I will discuss later.

WHEN GRIEVING, TWO PEOPLE ARE RARELY ON THE SAME GRIEF SCHEDULE.

I've noticed that, like life, grief is also like a river. The wave of the current flows from the trough to the crest and then back down to the trough again. If you have enough self-awareness of this, and especially if you're taking notes along the journey, you can begin to recognize your current water level and anticipate the rise and fall. While feeling pretty good and breathing fresh air, you can identify your crest. After time—sometimes minutes, sometimes days—when you feel a slight drop in your stability, you can expect the continued fall into the trough where the world seems dark, closed in, and meaningless. The great thing about this realization is knowing that neither the crest nor the trough lasts forever. In the trough you can cry the tears and hold on for one tiny gasp of air at a time, but you ultimately know that soon the current will slowly lift you back up again. We have control of this knowledge, and there is comfort in that.

The problem occurs when stubborn guys, like me, believe we can control more than just the knowledge of life's river. We think we can also manipulate the rise and fall of the water current itself.

"The power is within you!" says self-help.

It took the dark night for me to come to grips with the fact that I actually have no control over the waves in the river at all. Pretending that we do, and fighting against the pressure, leads to so much fatigue that we don't even have enough energy to breathe at the crest. The Source of the river was something I still hadn't connected with, but I would soon.

In John 6:44 Jesus said, "No one can come to me unless the Father who sent me draws him." When the call came, it was irresistible.

THE SOURCE

One day my friend Bernie, after hearing about my Billy Graham bingeing, texted me a three-minute YouTube clip from a pastor named John Piper. I still have the text from February 27, 2020. The title of the video was "Popular Verses: A Video Devotional with John Piper—Day 5."[4]

RIGHT THERE IN THAT TRUCK ON A SMALL COUNTY ROAD IN TEXAS, THE OLD ME DIED.

Bernie texted, "Not sure if you listen or read much Piper, but this was pretty awesome. Enjoy the day, brother!"

I replied, "Never heard of him. I'll dive in!"

I liked the video a lot. Piper had a different flow than Graham, and that spoke to me. I went searching for whatever else this guy had to offer and found more videos than my truck had miles to drive.

I remember the exact moment: the deep-blue color of an early spring sky, the grip of the steering wheel in my hands, and the exact stretch of blacktop and mile marker where it happened. It was March 1, 2020. I was listening to a Piper sermon on YouTube titled "How to Seek the Holy Spirit."[5]

At just before the forty-six-minute mark, Piper was reading from John 14:22–23 where one of Jesus' followers asked Him, "'Lord, how is it that you will manifest yourself to us, and not to the world?' Jesus answered him, 'If anyone loves me, he will keep my word, and my Father will love him, and we will come to him and make our home with him.'"

There was a pause. In deep, gut-wrenching conviction, Piper remarked, "That's not unconditional love. It is *profoundly conditional!*"

He reread the same text again. "*If anyone loves me, he will keep my word, and my Father will love him.*" After a pause, Piper again passionately interjected, "*In a way that He doesn't love everybody!*"

I can't fully explain what happened next, but suffice it to say that my eyes were opened to see things like never before. I was loved! I *felt* it. Not because of anything I had done. In fact, I certainly didn't deserve it, yet He had adopted me as a son. That revelation while hearing the gospel triggered a flood—not the hopeless flood I had felt after losing River but God's covenant flood of His Spirit to live in me and walk with me. I fell head over heels into an unprompted, unrehearsed, spontaneous prayer, without thinking about the words. I don't even fully remember what I said, but with tears like a river rushing down my cheeks, my prayer went something like this.

Jesus, save me! I want to seek You. I want to follow You. I want to learn You. I want to pursue You. I want to crave You. I want to desire You. Make me hunger for You, make me thirst for You, make me ache for You. Take my life, do as You please. I am Your servant, I am Your sheep, I am Your child . . . Jesus, I am Yours!

In that moment I was reborn!

Right there in that truck on a small county road in Texas, the old me died.

God had completely and irresistibly invaded my heart, and I was overflowing with gratitude. It was all His grace, which can be defined as unmerited favor. I suddenly hated living a life that wasn't pleasing to Him, but that's not what merited His love; instead, that was my *response* to it. I was a newly activated yet always predestined child of the one and only God, the uncompromising, unyielding, undeterred, all-knowing, all-determining, all-loving, almighty Creator of all things, the Source, and the Designer of my river from beginning to end. I was *His*, and that absolutely blew me away. I had known of God before, but now I understood something far greater than that: He knew *me*.

THE REAL MIRACLE MORNING

It was as though I had been handed a key that opened a door that had been locked, and when I gazed inside, nothing looked the same.

I went home and ditched the self-help books. I sidelined the devotionals, the visualizations, and the affirmations. I deleted the meditation apps and quit those cold turkey. I took the weed pen and all the oil and tossed them in the trash. I was certain of one thing now: I didn't need them anymore.

I dusted off my childhood Bible. I was starving for what it would feed to my wearied soul.

Where should I start?

I thought about it for a moment. Jesus had saved me on my darkest night. Billy Graham spoke of His death and unfathomable resurrection, but what else does Jesus say in here? I made my decision. "Okay. I'll just start at the birth of Christ, which is in the first book of the Bible's New Testament."

I turned to the first chapter of Matthew. I was holding a New International Version study Bible that began the chapter with an introductory commentary. I read every word and looked up every footnote. I was no longer a man drowning at the bottom of a river; I was a starving man who had just found bread, and I feasted on that bread, the Word of God, as if my life depended on it—because it did.

The more I ate at that table, the hungrier I grew. I combed over the words as if they were an instruction manual specifically written for my life. I didn't want to miss a single word from the God who had saved me. If I didn't understand something, I reread it. And then reread it again.

If I still didn't understand, I read the commentary in the NIV, or I searched YouTube for another educated resource.

I felt peace and joy and hope and purpose and became less dependent on *anything* else. My morning routine was drastically altered from a laundry list of self-help practices to now sipping a cup of coffee while continuing from the last place I had read in the Bible.

I was still grieving the loss of River, but now I was grieving with hope—hope that none of my pain was meaningless. None of it was wasted. All of it was purposeful. All this "light momentary affliction" was preparing me for an "eternal weight of glory beyond all comparison" (2 Corinthians 4:17). I could see that now.

I thought about my therapy retreat in Tennessee and the letter I wrote to the tree. I know God was planting the seeds of this real-life tree parable to me even back then. Consider this.

Every year a tree sheds its dead leaves. Some might hang on longer than others, but even those will eventually get pushed out by new growth. It's the process of rebirth. You might think that dead leaves are just wasted, but they are not. They're preparing the forest for what's to come. The fallen leaves decay on the ground and become nutrients for the soil, which is the lifeblood of the forest. If during this process the tree constantly focused on looking down at the soil and the dead leaves, then it would miss the source that causes the rebirth in the first place—the sun.

I had hidden my dark-night story from the world, but I no longer could. All of the pain, the struggle, the anxiety, the dead leaves from my tree had a purpose. I could see that now. Not only had Jesus rescued me from the bottom of the river, He had also fed this starving beggar. I was finally eating the Bread of Life and wanted to tell all the other beggars where I found it.

If you, too, are drowning in your own turbulent river and are still not sure where to go or what to do, flip to the back of this book. On a page titled "You Really, Really Need to Read This . . .", I've written a biblical understanding of how my rebirth was triggered. Check it out for yourself.

9

PEACE LIKE A RIVER

For thus says the Lord: "Behold, I will extend peace to her like a river, and the glory of the nations like an overflowing stream; and you shall nurse, you will be carried upon her hip, and bounced upon her knees."

Isaiah 66:12

PAIN IS NOT PERMANENT, AND it's not purposeless. Even in my darker times before God awakened me, I longed for this to be true. Don't we all to some extent? I believe that the desire to look for meaning in the ashes of tragedy comes programmed into our DNA because we were beautifully made in the image of our Creator.

All of us have stories where we've seen some kind of evidence that there was an unexplainable rhythm to this planet, things that lead us to believe there's an orchestrated purpose or design or destiny underlying our otherwise directionless existence. Many times we call it luck, karma, chance, a glitch in the Matrix, an accident, or a coincidence, but is that the correct way to define it?

When someone says, "It was meant to be," wouldn't the next logical question be "Meant to be by whom?" And then why would said designer make some things meant to be, but not all other things? I mean, if anything is meant to be, then naturally, aren't *all* things meant to be? If some things were meant to be and other things were left to chance, then wouldn't the things left to chance hinder the things set in stone and meant to be? That's a lot to think about. As I navigated the many months after my tragedy, these are questions I really needed to unpack. Over and over in my first passes through the Bible, those questions were answered in detail.

- "Many are the plans in the mind of a man, but it is the purpose of the LORD that will stand." (Proverbs 19:21)
- "The LORD of hosts has sworn: 'As I have planned, so shall it be, and as I have purposed, so shall it stand.'" (Isaiah 14:24)

- "I form light and create darkness; I make well-being and create calamity; I am the LORD, who does all these things." (Isaiah 45:7)
- "Declaring the end from the beginning and from ancient times things not yet done, saying, 'My counsel shall stand, and I will accomplish all my purpose.'" (Isaiah 46:10)
- "I know, O LORD, that the way of man is not in himself, that it is not in man who walks to direct his steps." (Jeremiah 10:23)
- "I know that you can do all things, and that no purpose of yours can be thwarted." (Job 42:2)
- "Who has spoken and it came to pass, unless the Lord has commanded it?" (Lamentations 3:37)
- "The LORD has made everything for its purpose." (Proverbs 16:4)
- "All the inhabitants of the earth are accounted as nothing, and he does according to his will among the host of heaven and among the inhabitants of the earth; and none can stay his hand or say to him, 'What have you done?'" (Daniel 4:35)
- "And we know that for those who love God all things work together for good, for those who are called according to his purpose." (Romans 8:28)

These verses are a few examples of the clear picture of God that is woven throughout all sixty-six books of the Bible. According to Scripture, the Source of the river is in complete control of everything that happens downstream.

If this is true, then the response to that knowledge could only be complete surrender, humility, and trust in His purpose. And instead of wasting our futile efforts fighting against the current, we are called to align ourselves with the flow.

And the result of that surrender?

Peace, joy, love, and hope. These are things I did not have at the time.

It doesn't mean there won't be any suffering; in fact, the Bible promises tribulation. But it allowed me to see that there's a meaningful reason behind all of it. Today, with my eyes wide open, I'm still discovering new reasons.

MINIATURE NAVY SEAL

I sensed this "glitch in the Matrix" many times after we lost Riv. But the first time was while we were still in the hospital.

During the first day and night I experienced a roller coaster of emotions—anxiety, confusion, panic, guilt, and shame—but I also felt something else: relief. From the moment the emergency responders recovered Riv's heartbeat, I knew he had a tough battle ahead of him, but I always thought he was going to make it. After all, River was a fighter. Even the doctors could sense that.

The kid was tough as nails. Maybe the toughest I've ever seen. We used to have these octagon combat matches on the netted trampoline with the three kids. The objective was simple—tackle the opponent for a point, with each kid trading off turns being the defender. I would stand in the middle as the referee to help prevent any unauthorized punching, scratching, or biting.

The kids *loved* this game.

Lincoln was two years older and about a foot taller than Riv. London was four years older and at least two feet taller. Nonetheless, River was an absolute force to be reckoned with. He was easily tossed around by his older siblings because of his size, but what he lacked in height and weight, he made up for in the grit of a D-day beach invader. He was impossible to deter, had locking arms like a grizzly bear, and simply would not quit battling. He would get banged around so many times that I'd try to call off the match, but then he would pitch a crying fit to stay in the fight for one more chance in the octagon, bruises and all.

He also had the determination of a miniature Navy SEAL. From the time he could crawl, he had youngest-child syndrome—fighting to keep up with his older siblings. Around one year of age he rode one of those tiny tricycles around the kitchen. I noticed then that his depth perception was uncanny. He could pedal at top speed but still turn around each corner without ever banging into a chair, wall, or the kitchen island. He soon graduated to a battery-powered mini tractor, but he constantly complained that it didn't go fast enough. Maybe, against my better judgment, I might have spliced some wires and swapped the 12-volt battery for a 24-volt battery to double the speed. Just maybe. Honestly, I'd never seen a kid exude more happiness than when I saw Riv hit the gas pedal on that hybrid toy tractor. Especially the first time. He contagiously giggled so hard that I couldn't stop laughing myself.

River was always seeking the next thrill, and Amber and I were constantly reprimanding him and setting boundaries when he would fly Mach 2 on that tractor through the woods, weaving in and out of trees while standing in balance with only one foot on the seat. When his adventures got out of hand, I had to disconnect the battery and put up with his agonizing cries.

Then he graduated again. We decided to get the kids a small two-seater go-kart with a throttle governor, body-harness seatbelt, and roll cage. That seemed safer than the redneck-rigged 24-volt tractor toy. River was too short to reach the pedals, so we figured he would just love riding around in the passenger seat with his older brother or sister driving.

I should've known River better than that.

He begged and moaned and cried until finally I gave in and

stuffed two pillows behind his back so that he could reach the pedals and drive. I would stand in the field and watch him take lap after lap along a big oval dirt track, with a massively disproportionate purple helmet on his shoulders, until either he ran out of fuel or the sun went down. What's crazy about this story is that he started doing this when he was still only two years old.

If any child had a solid chance of surviving a severe injury, it was River. That was the little boy I knew—always fighting, never relenting. The ambulance took him to a small hospital before they transferred him to Dell Children's Medical Center, which had more comprehensive pediatric care. Every nurse and every doctor who looked at him told us that he had a chance. It usually sounded something like, "He's really sick, and he's undergone some serious trauma, but there's still a chance at any time that he can wake up from it."

I had my doubts in the middle of the first night when the seizures started, but I never lost hope that he would open his brown eyes again, even when I learned that he would most likely suffer from moderate to severe brain damage. That's why the conversation with the neurologist at 11:00 a.m. on day two was such a shock.

He called us into the family waiting room, sat us down, took a minute to compose himself, and then very slowly and deliberately told us that our little boy had zero sign of brain activity. The life-support machine was the only thing keeping air in his lungs and a beat in his heart. He paused there on the couch with elbows on his knees and eyes glassy. He told us that as the parents, we would have to make the decision on when to disconnect life support.

I was so shocked that I didn't have any words except, "Are you . . . sure?"

He quietly replied, "One hundred percent sure." He waited for our response.

I asked him the only other question I could think of, "Would you disconnect your own son in this situation?"

At this point he broke his professional stance, and his eyes winced in heartbreak.

"I would," he choked.

My brother Tyler interjected from the corner of the room, "Wait, wait, what do you mean? We're talking about *Riv* here!"

With tears streaming down her cheeks, Amber could barely squeak out, "We would like to get a second opinion, please."

The doctor stood up and said, "Absolutely. I'll assemble a team to come down and start another evaluation."

A few hours later, a somber team of neurologists came in to deliver the same news for the second time. River had zero brain activity and zero chance of surviving. His lungs would soon take their last breath. It was not a matter of if, but when. That decision would be up to us.

THE HARDEST DECISION WE NEVER HAD TO MAKE

When we notified the rest of our family and friends, I immediately began receiving loving messages on my phone that all had a similar tone to them.

> Praying for you guys!
> Praying for a miracle!
> Wrapping your family in love, trusting in a miraculous healing from God!

Some messages were as bold and deliberate as "*Do not* unplug that child. God *will* heal him. But in order to fully display God's glory, you need to remove all shadow of a doubt. Disregard the doctor's advice and give God space to do His work."

Amber and I took a walk outside through the hospital serenity garden to get some fresh air. We prayed for miraculous healing because we believed that God could do that. I still believe that. We prayed that the doctors missed something and that River would wake up from his coma. The thought occurred to me that because this would be such a high-profile story, God could get so much glory with a healing that would echo around the world.

That's when I felt the first glitch in the Matrix.

It was as if God were saying, "*Don't tell Me how I get My glory.*"

All at once it occurred to me that we were asking the wrong prayer. In our time of desperation we were only pleading for our own earthly desires. We never considered God's will. We were praying for control of our own boat in the immediate turbulence, but we never once asked for harmony with the river's Source.

This was many months before my rebirth that I shared with you. Still, the message was delivered to me clearly. I grabbed Amber and cried out what might have been the first *real* prayer of my life. It was not prompted by my own understanding, and it went something like this.

> *God, You alone are in control. You will receive the glory for this, according to Your purpose, not mine. You know my deepest desire—please heal this little boy! But give me strength in this moment to rest in Your plan, even if You don't perform this miracle. Give me the clarity I need to lead my wife and my kids on the journey ahead. Give me the wisdom I need to make this decision for River. I don't want it. I'm scared to death of it, but You*

have willed it, so I'll trust that You'll carry me through it. We can't do this on our own. We need You, God!

After that prayer there was no gust of wind or thunderbolt in the sky. I wasn't overwhelmed with peace either, but I did regain just enough God-given strength to walk back into the fire and discern the most difficult decision of my life. Inside, the doctor was waiting for our answer. That's when Amber unexpectedly threw a wrench into the entire dilemma, saying, "I want to donate his organs."

The doctor nodded, "Hmm. In that case, we'll need to keep his body alive until viable recipients are found, which will take at least another twenty-four hours. But I have to warn you that his brain is deteriorating quickly, and if he goes brain dead before we locate someone, the chance of harvesting certain organs will be lost."

I looked at Amber. We both knew that through our total surrender, God had answered the doctor's question for us. The hardest decision of our lives was one that we never had to make. The life support machine stayed plugged in that day.

RETURNING TO THE PAIN

A month later I felt another glitch in the Matrix. A dear friend called me while I was on tour with my family. He and his family were very invested in our story.

"How are you?" he asked.

"We're making it day by day, brother," I replied.

He began to cry on the other end of the phone. "I'm so embarrassed!" he said. "Here I am calling you, and yet I'm the one breaking down on the phone. And I don't even know why!"

He explained, "My son is River's age, and now every time

I hold him, I feel so much sadness because of your story. I can't stop thinking about it. I just can't imagine what you guys went through, and for some reason, it's hitting me extra hard."

In August 2019, just a few weeks after that phone call, my friend and his family went to his nephew's sixth birthday party at a community swimming pool. Because of River's story, with so many young children around the water, the adults were on high alert. When it was time to eat the cake, everyone was called over to the table. My friend did one more sweep to make sure no kids were left behind.

At some point during the brief moment of cutting the cake and blowing out the candles, the six-year-old's younger brother slipped away from the group and silently fell into the pool. He was discovered only moments later, but it was already too late.

The EMS recovered his heartbeat and rushed him off to Dell Children's Medical Center, the same hospital where we had taken River.

My friend called me again in desperation, this time to tell me about his nephew. I listened, gave him my sympathy, hung up, and told Amber, "We have to go there to be with them." She agreed.

Every mile down that same highway, and every step down that same pediatric intensive care unit hallway, was absolutely brutal. We passed the same nurses, walked through the same *Little Mermaid*–painted glass doors, and saw the same inconsolable look on the parents' faces. We made it to the little boy's room and found the same blankets and breathing-machine tubes in his nose. He was peaceful and beautiful, just as though he were sleeping.

My friend pulled me aside, "Granger, shoot me straight. The doctors are saying he might pull out of this, but I need to hear it from you for my brother's sake. Is he going to make it or not?"

I couldn't answer with words. I slowly shook my head no.

The family was gathering for a prayer circle. "Granger, would you and Amber join us in prayer, please?"

Amber and I quickly joined hands with them in the middle of the hallway. Each family member went around the circle and pleaded for God's mercy and complete healing. When the circle came around to me, there I was again, overwhelmed by God's clear and powerful sovereign presence. I spoke:

> *Oh God, we desperately want You to heal this child. You are a miracle worker, and You absolutely have the power. But give this family the strength and peace to rest in Your will, not ours. We trust whatever Your plan is today. And we will rejoice, even through our deepest sorrow, knowing that Your purpose is far greater than ours. Sometimes sickness is for healing, and other times it's for homecoming. We beg for healing today. But if You don't heal this boy on earth, heal the hearts of this family.*

A few hours later, my friend's three-year-old nephew passed away. I don't know why God called us back to the same hospital so soon after our loss. I don't know why I was given the words to repeat that same prayer through another impossible situation. I don't even know if it resonated with the grief-stricken family.

What I do know is that I was becoming sensitive to ideas that were not originating from my own understanding. My whole life I witnessed my mother speak as a mouthpiece for God, but she was a saint, and I certainly wasn't.

This was the first time I felt like God was calling me to a platform to use our story for His glory. I still didn't fully understand what it meant to surrender my life to the Source, but I did know this: my pain had a purpose.

You have to understand that this was not the plan I'd made for my life. The public platform I was so busy building wasn't based on anything spiritual, unless you see God through a cracked windshield, a backroad, and a pickup truck. Okay, I'll admit, there is something spiritual about that too.

MY PAIN HAD A PURPOSE.

When we try to keep living on our own, we won't have the strength to persevere through hardship. But when we, like a river, connect to the greater Source, when we surrender our lives to God and let the gospel take root in our hearts, we will be able to keep flowing downstream.

When that happens, life looks less like struggling and more like surrendering.

God uses us to help others, and when we do, we experience a peace that surpasses understanding—peace like a river.

That wasn't the last time I felt lead by the Spirit, and I wasn't finished standing on the new platform that He had given me. Not because I decided to but because soon I would be compelled to by His irresistible calling. I ran from it, I hid from it, I convinced myself during those dark days and nights that I absolutely wasn't qualified for it. But in a few months, I would hear His voice again, and this time He placed something on my heart that I never would've expected.

River's legacy story was only just beginning.

10

THE PHOENIX

Then the angel showed me the river of the
water of life, bright as crystal, flowing from
the throne of God and of the Lamb.

Revelation 22:1

WHEN THE SUMMER OF 2019 turned to fall and then the fall turned into winter, I had an extremely vulnerable and guilt-stricken thought. The thought was recurring, and eventually I was completely overcome with it.

Someday we would have another baby.

I felt so guilty about that idea that even the thought of entertaining it made me shudder. How selfish could I be? River was our baby boy! Was it unfaithful to him to even have thoughts like this?

Still, what might best summarize the feeling I had at the time would be this: I have more love to give. But my insecurities in all of it forced me to keep it to myself for weeks.

So I told no one. That is, until one night I dropped the idea on Amber.

I stumbled my way through a very vulnerable conversation. I said, "Uh, would you ever consider trying for another baby?"

She looked at me somberly and answered without hesitation, "No."

"I know, I know," I said. "But it's been on my heart lately, and I needed to bring it up to you just in case you were thinking the same thing, even though I didn't want to upset you by mentioning it."

"River was our last baby. He was always supposed to be," she told me with eyes full of tears. I honored that.

I honored my grieving wife.

I dismissed those tugging thoughts.

But a few nights later, she approached me saying, "If you have a strong feeling about this, then I should at least call my doctor and ask about options."

As I mentioned in chapter 2, after River was born, Amber and I were so certain that our family was complete that we elected to have her fallopian tubes tied to seal the deal. That was a foolish decision that I don't recommend to anyone. You never know what the future holds, and you can't pretend to know where the river is taking your boat.

Like many families, we had been planners since the beginning of our relationship. At our wedding shower, when asked how many kids we would like to have, our answer was unified: three plus one. Honestly, we didn't know exactly what that meant, but it was a good answer to keep the door open for possibly fostering or adopting.

In a few days, she got her answer back from the doctor. It would be extremely difficult whichever path we took. The odds were stacked high against it. She was thirty-nine years old, her tubes were tied, and she had undergone three previous cesarean sections due to carrying the first baby, London, completely breach in the womb—a pregnancy that without modern medicine would've killed her. Those are three bad strikes.

We had two options. One was tubal reversal surgery, which was risky, difficult, and expensive, with only a few doctors who could or even would do it.

We could also try in vitro fertilization (IVF), which, again, had a low success rate and was very expensive. But there were a few local clinics that would administer it. However, with IVF as the only real option, Amber cried heavy tears. "How dare we play God and create a baby in a test tube? It just doesn't feel right." I agreed. The discussion was over.

TREES AND SEEDS

To clear my head, I took the kids camping. This was the same night that I shared with you in chapter 6 when I made the mad barefoot dash to Wildflower to stop the slideshow.

The next morning we packed up and were driving to a small café for breakfast. Through the bitter cold, beautifully clear morning we drove down the backroads of central Texas. For miles in every direction were cornfields turned over to cover crop for the winter. This country is *flat*, and as the sun peeked over the plowed rows, we saw nothing but an endless horizon in every direction.

Lincoln was in the back seat of my pickup truck staring out the window. In his perfectly pure and innocent voice he asked the most random question: "Daddy, does God make some of the trees and man make some of the trees?" I was caught off guard by the obscure and profound question but even more surprised when I answered suddenly without any thought at all, "No, buddy. God makes *all* the trees. But sometimes man has to plant the seed."

I paused. What in the world? That was bizarre. It was like those weren't *my* words. They just fell out. I can't explain what that felt like or how strange it was.

Later, back at home, Amber and I were sitting cross-legged on the bed. The new baby discussion resumed, and once again Amber was crying. She confessed that she, too, had been thinking about the idea and was overrun with guilt. She cried, "I know that there's a slim chance with IVF, but I just . . . I can't do it! I can't wholeheartedly plant a baby seed in my womb. Who are we to play God?"

All at once it hit me. My eyes closed as tears ran down my cheeks.

I knew it.

All of it.

I knew God's answer for her.

For us.

For our family.

I whispered over the lump in my throat, "God makes all the babies. But sometimes man has to plant the seed."

Nothing more was said. There was nothing else that needed to be said. God had spoken definitively and clearly. He was doing a new thing.

We mapped out a plan, scheduled an introductory appointment at the fertility clinic in January 2020, and proceeded blindly in trusting surrender. Obedient to a purpose far greater than we could understand, we began our new journey, but it was never smooth sailing. All the earthly odds were not in our favor, but that didn't matter anymore. The Source of the river was.

Amber had fourteen viable eggs harvested; twelve fertilized correctly, and only seven made it to day six. Out of those, only two survived for transfer. The final two embryos were frozen in cryogenic storage. When the genetics were analyzed, both were boys.

Amber began a regimen of vitamins and enormous hormone shots to prepare her body for the implant. And we prayed.

Our prayers were not just, *God, give us a baby.* He already knew that's what we wanted. Instead, we prayed,

> *God, You are sovereign. You know the end from the beginning. We surrender to Your purpose and not ours. No seed grows without Your living water. If this is selfish, stop it. If this is an act of closure for us to rest with these questions about the finality of our family, so be it. But if it's a baby, we lay him at Your feet. He is Yours.*

Heal our hearts and humble us because the glory is all Yours regardless. Steady the hands of these doctors, and prepare Amber's womb in a way that only You can. Let Your will be done!

And then our earthly odds decreased again.

In March, COVID-19 ravaged the world, and soon the clinic went into lockdown for the first time in its existence. Many heartbroken, aspiring mothers, including Amber, were called with the devastating news: all IVF processes had stopped for the foreseeable future.

I couldn't imagine a clearer answer to our prayers. It seemed as though a worldwide pandemic that halted all medical procedures was an obvious sign that this was *not* the right path.

God had spoken again.

DEER, RABBITS, AND HONEYBEES

All my touring and traveling stopped. COVID was a huge distraction, and maybe that also allowed us to be more patient through such an intense season for us. Although continually searching for a new house was highly discouraged in our therapy retreat in Tennessee, I still was not able to comfortably settle into the temporary home where we lived, and I continued my compulsion of surfing real estate apps on my phone. That ended in April 2020.

The first time I laid eyes on the red barn and old windmill, I knew it was calling my name. On a real estate app, I found a little farm about thirty minutes away that seemed absolutely perfect. One afternoon I took a drive to check it out with my own eyes.

On the property were two barns, a beautiful old windmill, a water well, countless old live oak trees, and blankets of Texas wildflowers. I saw thick woods, open fields, deer, rabbits, honeybees, and many species of birds. My heart sailed!

It was simply perfect. It had everything I loved about the land where River had lived but without the bad memory. For the first time in a long time, I felt home.

I scrambled to call Amber. “Babe, what are you doing? Can you meet me out here?”

When she arrived, her reaction was the same as mine, except she had one pretty good question. “Umm, where is the house?”

I walked out into a field of bluebonnets tucked away under the shady oaks and stretched my arms out. “We’d have to build one, right here.”

Our eyes met, and she spoke clearly, “I love it. Let’s do it.”

God was doing something new, again.

I called the listing Realtor, and she said, “Oh, that ol’ place? We’re taking it off the market because of all this crazy COVID stuff.”

I snapped back, “Tell them we’ll pay full price. And we don’t want to change anything.”

She replied in a lower tone, “But there’s no house on the property. Don’t you want to take soil samples and inspect the well?”

I answered, “No. I can deal with all that after we close.” The sellers decided to accept our offer and set a closing date for early summer. Amber and I were now the happy owners of a little strip of farmland: half pasture, half wooded with two barns, a windmill, and no house.

God was now guiding my boat.

“While you build, rent a house and live there temporarily!” said everyone.

Contrary to the advice of our friends, I convinced Amber that we should park an RV in one of the barns and live there for the year it would take to build.

Amber used to be much more indecisive. She needed to completely weigh the pros and cons ahead of every big decision. Now she looked at life through a different lens. Losing River had given her a new perspective to the tune of "tomorrow is not guaranteed." She believed we needed to live life as presently and as purposefully as possible. A new adventure, experiencing all four seasons with all of us confined into a small area, seemed like really good medicine for our family. So that's what we did.

We borrowed a really nice Grand Design RV from Explore USA. The kids were absolutely ecstatic! It had one master bedroom in the front, a kitchen in the middle, and a back bedroom with four small bunk beds. The great thing was that the barn already had a small restroom with a shower, so we didn't need to hook up the water and plumbing. Instead, we used the two small RV restrooms as closets, hanging our clothes on the sliding shower doors.

In the barn itself we set up couches, a coffee table, and a TV. Our dogs slept on pet beds under the RV, our chickens pecked around and gave us a constant supply of eggs from the coop outside, and our two fainting goats grazed the green grass around the property. (Yes, they faint when scared. Look them up. It's hysterical!)

It was a pretty sweet setup that I'll never forget. My gut instinct was right. This new adventure was exactly what the family needed. In fact, the kids said it was their favorite house they had ever lived in.

It wasn't all peaches and cream, however. We quickly adapted to barn life and learned that the deer, rabbits, and honeybees weren't as plentiful as the rattlesnakes, scorpions, and giant wolf spiders that carried hundreds of babies on their backs. Evidently we weren't the only ones who loved that barn.

One of the kids' many chores was vacuuming up dead roly-polies (a.k.a. pill bugs) that seemed to visit us by the thousands every day. In one of my journal entries during that time, I wrote, "Hey, future self, how do you like living in a real house? Never forget the roly-polies."

The dogs stayed busy chasing off skunks, armadillos, possums, raccoons, and the occasional bat that flew under the barn door. All critters loved our barn.

But it wasn't anything with legs, scales, or wings that created our biggest challenge back then. It was the brutal Texas heat. It could easily get up to 110 degrees midday inside the barn. We learned to pattern our lives around the elements and the weather, which was something so nostalgic, so primal, and so healing. When it rained on that thin tin roof, we felt it. When the thunder clapped and rattled those aluminum walls, we were shaken by it. And when the sun burned hot, we couldn't escape it. We were totally aligned with God and His creation.

Those true miracle mornings, sitting outside before the sun came up with my bare feet in the soil, were some special moments that I'll never forget. They shaped my newly reborn soul.

I finished my first complete read of the Bible out there. I rattled around and contemplated deep theology and the meaning of life. I built a small vegetable garden, and while tending to and watering the tomatoes, cucumbers, okra, corn, potatoes, and peppers, I prayed some of my deepest, most heartfelt prayers.

There was one prayer that I repeated more than any other. I was praying for those two tiny frozen embryos that were locked away in a freezer in an abandoned fertility clinic in Austin, Texas.

THE UNEXPLAINABLE DREAM

In early June 2020, around River's Angel Day (that's what we call the day River went to be with Jesus), the clinic called to say that they were resuming IVF procedures with all patients. We entered with determined and hopeful hearts, and they gave us a new target implant date, and Amber restarted her intense vitamin and hormone shot regimen. With our approval, based on a DNA grading system that ranked one embryo with a higher probability of implantation success than the other, the doctors chose one of the embryos.

Several weeks later, we made the tearful, hopeful, prayerful drive to Austin for the transfer procedure. I watched the unbelievable images from a scoped camera displaying on a screen in another room as they gently pressed the tiny cluster of a baby into Amber's uterus.

Incredible.

As the doctor removed her latex gloves, she came into my room and said, "Well, she did great! Everything looks as it should. Now we wait. In a week and a half bring her back in. If the implant was a success, she'll be six weeks pregnant."

Those were probably the longest ten days of my life.

The kids had absolutely no idea what we were doing, but one morning something unexplainable happened. Lincoln came into breakfast, hair all messed up and eyes puffy from sleeping.

"Mommy, I had a dream last night that River was with me."

Amber paused, "Aww sweetie, what did he say?"

Lincoln replied, "He told me everything was going to be all right."

Amber smiled, "I love that. I believe he's right. Everything *is* going to be all right."

Lincoln paused for a second. "And another thing, Mommy . . . he told me that you were having another baby."

Amber was speechless and fumbled for her phone and hit Record on the voice recorder. "Um. Wow! Okay. Well, did he tell you what the baby was?"

Lincoln didn't hesitate. "Yes. A brother. Another baby brother."

We listened to that phone recording over and over again. We just couldn't understand it. How was that possible?

Only God.

When the long week was finally over, Amber went alone to the clinic for a pregnancy test. She returned to the barn while we waited for the phone call to confirm the results.

"Here it is!" She shouted as the phone rang, and I ran to be with her. She put the call on speakerphone.

"Hi, Amber? Yes, we have your results. Congratulations! You're pregnant with a baby boy!"

Standing there in the heat of the barn with the roly-polies and the spiders, we were suddenly and completely overwhelmed by every possible emotion: joy, relief, gratitude, thankfulness, and of course, sadness. In that moment, as we held each other, the tears of joy were indistinguishable from the tears of grief. It was a miracle, and God had His fingerprints all over it.

THE TEARS OF JOY WERE INDISTINGUISHABLE FROM THE TEARS OF GRIEF.

A few weeks later, we went back to the clinic. For the first time we heard the beautiful heartbeat as we watched the tiny boy with two arms and two legs dance around on the sonogram. On the way home we decided that it was time to tell the kids. Although they had graduated from months of play therapy and had done very well, there were still occasional and understandable sad moments dealing with the memory of River. We knew that this would be the best news they had heard in at least a year. They needed that spirit boost, and as expected, they were overwhelmed with happiness when we told them. They giggled over baby names, wondered about eye and hair color, and negotiated who would give up space in their bedroom for a new crib.

On August 19, Amber went alone for the baby's graduation appointment while I headed to Wildflower for a short weekend tour. At the fertility clinic, *graduation* meant this was the final visit until we moved on to the ob-gyn and the delivery hospital.

"Welcome to graduation day!" The nurses met her with applause and cheers. They knew just how long our journey had been to get to this day, and we felt grateful to the core. So many couples struggle with infertility, and IVF has a very low success rate. We were extremely blessed, and that was not lost on us.

The doctor flicked on the screen in the dimly lit room and began inspecting Amber with the probe.

"Okay, let's see, ahh, there he is."

"Hmm."

"Oh no."

"I'm so sorry. He no longer has a heartbeat."

"I am so, so sorry."

The bus hadn't driven away from the office when Amber texted me: "Have you left yet?"

I replied: "Not yet, what's up?"

Amber quickly responded: "I'm coming there."

That wasn't good. She wouldn't have wanted to drive out there unless . . .

No.

Surely not.

Amber pulled up to the bus and stepped out. Her face said it all. Without saying a word, she shook her head.

When she began to cry, I didn't. I couldn't feel anything really.

I was just confused. This couldn't be. Why would this happen to us? What was the point of the vision God gave me? How about the seeds and the tree revelation? Or Lincoln's dream? None of it made any sense. I couldn't have misunderstood this. My message from God was more real than anything I'd ever experienced.

Then, suddenly, like a lightning strike on a metal barn, I was snapped out of my trance by the next thought.

There was still one more frozen embryo.

THE DESTINY OF OUR FAMILY

The miscarriage was an absolute defining moment for Amber. She placed her entire trust in God, regardless of what the future might bring. She elected to have the miscarriage naturally, and we decided not to tell the kids until the end of the entire process, baby or not. We needed to protect their hearts; that was a roller coaster they didn't need to ride. The news of losing the baby was devastating, but it also gave resolution to another problem we were wrestling with.

What would happen with the second embryo if the first one worked? There were four options: donate to science, donate to another mother, dispose, or implant. Amber and I had decided that we would consider the last option, even though she would be at least forty-one years old by that time and a fifth cesarean surgery was very risky.

It's honestly a blessing that we never had to fight that battle; God did.

I will never be able to explain, or even begin to understand, the miscarriage itself. But what I know is that Amber was in tremendous pain—both physically and emotionally. The process took fifteen days, two of those lying on towels on the concrete bathroom floor in the barn while I distracted our kids, keeping them away from the door.

"Is Mommy okay? Is the baby okay?" they repeatedly asked me.

I would reassure them by saying, "Mommy is a little sick right now. God is in complete control of both her and the baby. Would y'all like to pray again for them?"

After it was over, Amber emerged like a phoenix from the ashes, a completely different woman. She was calm, collected, courageous, and confident in God's promise, regardless of the outcome. There was no more anxiety and no more worry. She had completely surrendered to the Source of the river and was allowing the current to carry her without resistance. It was beautifully inspiring, like when precious metals are refined by fire.

It would take six weeks for her body to fully recover for a second implantation, but this time she flipped the script.

"I've decided that this time I'm not going to take any vitamins or hormone shots. I want my body to prepare naturally. If God has plans for another baby, I'll leave that completely up to Him. If not, I'll trust Him anyway, and we'll have absolute closure for the rest of our lives that River was our last biological baby."

She was resolute, and I agreed.

Either way, soon enough we would know the destiny of our family.

11

THE MAVERICK

"Behold, I am doing a new thing; now it springs
forth, do you not perceive it? I will make a way
in the wilderness and rivers in the desert."

Isaiah 43:19

THERE WAS A LOT OF freedom in those six weeks prior to embryo transfer number two. Ironically, the rest of the world was in lockdown, which meant our touring was at a complete standstill. Every concert on the books was either canceled or rescheduled, and most of those rescheduled events eventually went away forever. Music, a big part of my life that had once helped distract me from my grief, was now buried inside an even bigger distraction—how to keep my band and crew on salary and provide health insurance for their families.

We played live stream concerts for tips, my bus drivers and I made monetized YouTube videos recording the complete restoration of my dad's old 1974 GMC pickup (the one with the missing door), but more than anything, we doubled down on our commitment to our e-commerce brand, Yee Yee Apparel. It certainly was a different kind of show to see the band and crew members packing and shipping merchandise.

During this time something else also got a face-lift—the *Granger Smith Podcast*. Although in the years prior I had occasionally uploaded storytelling episodes, I made a commitment to produce and release new episodes every Monday morning. And in order to keep churning out continuous content, I decided that instead of the traditional storytelling, I would answer questions from the listeners that they could submit by email. This reduced my prep time for each show but also gave me a platform to walk through complicated life situations with people based on my own experiences and through a biblical worldview. I didn't always have the right answers, and I certainly wasn't a psychologist, but I could always point them toward the Source of the river, and that direction was always right. As I've said many times on the podcast, I'm just one beggar telling another beggar where I found bread.

I'M JUST ONE BEGGAR TELLING ANOTHER BEGGAR WHERE I FOUND BREAD.

Turning the mirror around on the listeners and meticulously navigating their diverse questions allowed the podcast to soar in popularity. Given my rocky past and my questionable, un-saintlike history, I felt neither qualified nor worthy of that success—a testament to the Lord, not the sinner, growing the platform.

All these things would not have been possible without COVID shaking the dead leaves off my tree.

It's hard to know how I would've handled losing my son and my touring career in less than one year if I hadn't gone through such a radical transformation. After that, I understood that whatever happened was going to happen and that *everything* that happens from here on out is part of a greater purpose that is *always* laced with meaning.

Like the dead leaves of a tree in autumn, nothing is wasted.

In chapter 8 I shared the story of my rebirth in the truck. That happened on March 1, 2020. COVID began to shut down the United States on March 12. Coincidence? By now you probably know that I don't believe in coincidences. No longer was I fighting the river rapids. Instead, I realized that I had been given just enough air in my lungs to keep me floating along with the current.

When Jesus taught His disciples how to pray, He said, "Give us this day our daily bread" (Matthew 6:11). I've often wondered why He didn't just give us bread that would last a lifetime. I've come to realize that we *need* to be renewed day by day. It's how we're wired. The longer we drive around with a full fuel tank, the longer we don't need to refuel at the station. And the longer we stay away from the station, the less connected we are with the Source. And when we become disconnected from the Source, well, hopefully by now you can see where I'm going with this.

I saw both the good and the bad things in my journey differently now. So did Amber.

IMPOSSIBLE ODDS

My 2020 distractions weren't only work related. Living in the barn, we endured one of the hottest summers ever on record in Texas, which would soon turn into one of the coldest winters. The slab was poured on our new house in October, and nail by nail, board by board, we watched with reassurance that one day we'd once again have real air-conditioning and running water in a kitchen.

Life in a barn with two adults, two kids, two dogs, two goats, one cat, fifteen chickens, two beehives, a worm farm, and fifty million roly-polies was *always* an adventure. And we were fully present for all of it.

On one of the rare tour dates at Lake of the Ozarks in Missouri, I picked up another surprise for the kids. Maybe I was subconsciously already preparing them for disappointment if we didn't have a baby. Maybe I was trying to lift Amber's spirits after miscarrying the first baby. Maybe I just like punishing myself—I don't know. But I brought home another puppy from that trip: our third dog and our second German shorthaired pointer from Whoa Nelly's Kennel, a female named Luna. As expected, the kids went crazy, and Dad scored some major brownie points.

Amber took a few trips back to Austin for checkups at the clinic. They would inspect her uterus with a camera to make sure the miscarriage had completely cycled through and that there were no changes in her health, in preparation for the final embryo transfer. The doctors were informed about her unorthodox decision to forgo hormone shots and vitamins, and Amber was undeterred. This would happen as naturally as possible.

As we learned from the first failed pregnancy, the statistics were stacked high against making a baby from a test tube. The probability of a woman between the age of thirty-eight and forty carrying full term in a pregnancy with IVF is 26.7 percent.[6] With those odds, I wouldn't wager anything of value. But as Jesus said in Matthew 19:26, "With man this is impossible, but with God all things are possible."

As the husband, I had no more than a support role in this process, so I asked her multiple times if she really wanted to go through with this for a second time. I was worried not only about the physical pain of another miscarriage but also about the emotional defeat she would inevitably endure as well, all for the sake of my strong desire for another baby. She wouldn't hear any of it. She was a hardened soldier now.

She looked me dead in the eye with incredible courage and determination and said, "No. We will see this through. I believe now that you were right all along: God has a plan for another baby in this family."

On December 8 we drove the well-traveled path back to Austin to the fertility clinic for the second and final implant. The last remaining one from the seven original embryos had been in cryo freeze now for eleven months.

That day's transfer went similar to the first.

Everything went as planned.

Everything was normal.

We drove home with the newly thawed cluster of cells in Amber's belly, prayed along the way, and started the ten-day waiting period before we would hear back whether it was successful.

The kids still had no idea that any of this was happening. Lincoln was overwhelmed with joy and oblivious, but London was very inquisitive, "Mommy, why is your belly not growing yet?"

She counted on her fingers. "One, two, three, four months. You're four months pregnant. Why don't you have a little pooch in your belly yet?"

We answered the only way we felt was appropriate and correct, "In God's timing, when He wants the baby to grow, He'll make the baby grow."

We both knew that we couldn't hold back information from our very bright nine-year-old much longer. As soon as we felt it was appropriate, we would tell her everything.

THE UNBRANDED CALF

We decided that during the waiting period, we should think of a name for the baby and involve the kids. We wanted River's legacy running through all of it.

Because London and Lincoln were both named after towns in England where Amber's family was from, I scanned a list of British names, looking for their meaning, and I found one: Beckham. It meant "home by the river." It was a perfect middle name, but what about the first?

Amber wanted to find a name that had the letters *R*, *I*, and *V* in it. We racked our brains for what that could be, and then one day it hit us—Maverick.

The name originates from a nineteenth-century Texan named Samuel A. Maverick, who allowed his cattle to roam around unbranded. Soon the name became synonymous with unbranded livestock. By the end of the 1800s, the name *Maverick* referred to individuals who prefer to blaze their own trails.[7] It was the perfect name for a little trailblazer, our little unbranded calf. It surely didn't hurt that my favorite childhood movie was *Top Gun*, and at one time I had every line of the film memorized. Amber loved the name because it contained the letters *R*, *I*, and *V*, a forever connection with his older brother.

Mirroring the first transfer, on the tenth day we received a call from the clinic that confirmed Amber was once again pregnant. This time we harnessed our emotions and remained optimistic that God's plan would be fully revealed in the weeks to come. On January 7, 2021, we heard the heartbeat for the first time, strong and fast. We decided it was time to sit the kids down and tell them the whole story.

"Guys, Mommy and Daddy heard Maverick's heartbeat today, and he's doing great."

They grinned and giggled with excitement.

"But the reason Mommy's belly isn't showing any signs of a baby yet is because this is a different baby than when we first told you. We don't know why God does certain things, but we always trust Him that He knows what is best and we don't. We also don't know whether this baby will make it or not, but we can sure pray that he does. Either way we'll praise God for all the blessings He has given us."

London and Lincoln sat in deep thought.

"So if this is Maverick, then what was the other baby's name?" London asked.

That was a good question. We didn't have a name for him.

Lincoln chimed in, "I want to name him Noah. I love Noah."

We smiled at his innocent heart and replied, "I think Noah is a great name, buddy."

London asked, "So what is Maverick's due date?"

Amber said, "August."

London wrinkled her forehead, "August? Ugh, that's so long! I want to meet him now!"

I told her, "Sissy, if this is God's plan, then our house will be finished by then, and it will be perfect timing. You'll meet him before you know it."

She smiled and kissed Amber's belly.

On January 19, exactly one year from the very first time we visited the clinic, Amber wasn't alone for the graduation day.

This time I went with her.

The sonogram probe didn't take long to find baby Maverick. We both cried as we watched on the screen as a tiny human danced in her womb, sporting a healthy, vibrant heartbeat.

This visit was different from any other we had made over the past year. As we exited down the long hallway, we ran our fingers across all the painted baby footprints decorating the walls. So many babies. But those footprints represented only a drop in the bucket compared to the countless parents who had walked away from the clinic with shattered hopes and empty wombs. It was humbling and sobering. We would not take this blessing for granted, not for one second.

Man can plant the seed, but only God grows the tree.

WHEN THE TREE FALLS

The news of this pregnancy didn't negate or replace the heaviness we still felt for our loss of River. We continued to have our ups and downs that were natural in the waves of grief. And none of it was a distraction from the tremendous love we had for London and Lincoln. Through it all, we were discovering new depths in our emotional capacity.

What we learned was that grief and joy can beautifully coexist.

I'm not saying you can be sad and happy at the same time; that's not what I mean. Consider this. Happiness happens to you. It's something you feel when things are going well. It's temporary. But joy is different. It's an internal peace, a gift that can never be replaced or taken away, which means it can exist even alongside our deepest sorrow. We were still hurting, but we were also joyful even in our circumstances, and that birthed a hope within us—a hope that wasn't fruitless. After Amber's and my complete and painful surrender, it was becoming evident that God was doing something new. He was restoring us—not by removing the fire but by walking us right through the middle of it.

WHAT WE LEARNED WAS THAT GRIEF AND JOY CAN BEAUTIFULLY COEXIST.

In February, when Amber was three months pregnant, the band's touring was still completely shut down. While the future of my career was still uncertain, the weather was forecasting one of the worst Texas cold fronts in recorded history, and the storm hit our little farm with a vengeance.

First the temperature dropped down into the high twenties. Next came the heavy rains. I'm no meteorologist, but I've never seen heavy raindrops pouring down while the temp is below freezing, but that's exactly what happened. Texas live oak trees are evergreen, so they don't lose their leaves during the winter.

Every time a raindrop hit a tree leaf, it immediately stuck and froze solid. As it continued to rain relentlessly, the branches grew heavier and heavier with every drop that turned to ice. By the time the rain stopped, the damage was already done. The beautiful, old live oaks could not take the intense strain, and their branches and trunks began to break.

The once-quiet evening now sounded like a war zone with snaps, pops, cracks, and exploding branches echoing throughout the woods. Even the ground under my feet would rumble when somewhere in the near distance a massive tree or limb slammed onto the earth.

Phase two of the storm brought the snow, heavy and thick like I've seen only in the northern states. Several feet deep in places, it packed on top of the ice and blanketed the trees that were still standing but bent over, hanging on for dear life.

And then came phase three, the bitter cold. For the first time that any Texan could remember, the temperature dropped all the way down below zero degrees Fahrenheit.

With so many people running their heaters on high, the Texas power grid failed, causing the electricity to be cycled on and off in order to distribute it. The cold penetrated the barn, and snow found its way into every tiny slit under and between the doors. We slept in our clothes, piled on blankets, and cooked frozen venison meat on our carefully rationed propane stove inside the RV. On day four our water well froze solid, but I was anticipating that and had filled several five-gallon jugs of water before we lost it.

Since we were so far out in the country, we had no cell service, and with no power, we didn't have Wi-Fi either. There was no way to communicate with the outside world.

I ventured out a few times in my four-wheel-drive truck, but the roads were slick like glass. The countryside looked apocalyptic. I could make it only a few miles in any direction before

I'd end up finding someone stranded in a ditch. I'd pull them out with chains, deliver food to neighbors who couldn't leave the house, and then return home to preserve fuel. We really had no idea if this would last for another day or another week, or even whether the power grid would continue to function when the ground thawed. It was a once-in-a-lifetime storm, and it didn't relent for seven days.

When I tell my northern friends about this, they roll their eyes. So let me put it in perspective. Birds were literally falling out of the sky, and their dead bodies were scattered all over the frozen snow. Deer were dying. One-hundred-year-old trees were falling over or simply freezing to their eventual death. Even when wrapped, pipes were bursting all over the state because, for this kind of intense cold, nothing was properly buried. Texas is not Minnesota.

I stood on the icy ground looking around in the eerie silence of the forest. I thought about my conversation with the tree during my therapy retreat in Tennessee and about the irony of how I was now the one standing and watching fallen and broken trees. Dealing with the devastation that surrounded me would've been an impossible situation for a man who loves to paddle down his own river, but that wasn't me anymore. I bowed my head and closed my eyes.

God, whatever it is You're doing, I trust You, I prayed as trees crackled, split, and crashed down, taking along with them every other branch in their path like a German Panzer tank in the French countryside. *You brought me to this land. You knew that I would fall in love with these trees and wildlife, and now You're devastating it.*

I thought about my pregnant wife and two kids bundled up safely inside the RV. I thought about the miraculous journey we had taken up until that moment. My prayer deepened.

Don't allow me to covet things of this earth. It's all temporary and fleeting. Even when we plant the seeds, You grow the trees, and You, only You, decide how long they stand. Somewhere off in the woods another branch broke loose and plummeted into the snow, echoing through the quiet.

Give me new desires only for the eternal things, not the earthly ones. Increase my faith in You and not on my own understanding. Remove any illusion that this home is forever . . . because it's not. Once again, God, renew me.

And He did.

He renewed the land as well.

After the storm passed, the ground thawed, and the bright Texas sun began its work. The brilliant, warm sparkle turned the ice to beautiful droplets of water, freeing the leaves and branches of their heavy burden. The remaining branches that had held strong now bounced upward like tightly wound springs. Abrupt whooshing sounds filled the forest, no longer in devastation but with the sound of regained life.

As the seasons changed and as Amber's belly grew, clearing the land of the fallen foliage was part of my daily routine. Friends would come over with their chainsaws, and we'd cut the trees into smaller pieces. Trip after trip, we dragged the limbs to brush piles, and over and over we burned them down to ashes. The kids chipped in as well, carrying firewood and stacking the logs in tall piles by the barn. They grumbled daily as they dragged around a little red wagon full of wood, but I think they secretly loved the responsibility.

I don't think I'll *ever* have to worry about running out of firewood in my lifetime. With every chainsaw cut I made and every branch I carried to the brush pile, I thought about the ice storm and God's immutable providence through it all. Like the good

Father He is, He was always teaching me—sometimes by giving, sometimes by taking away, but always for His perfect purpose.

Don't allow me to covet the things of this earth, I prayed.

The storm taught me to never again take for granted a fresh budding leaf on a live oak tree, a tiny cardinal egg in the birdhouse, or a spotted baby fawn tucked away in the long grass. Though nothing was guaranteed, everything felt like a blessing.

WORTHLESS HANDS

As July rolled around and the scorching heat reassured us that Texas was definitely not Minnesota, Amber was ready for two things: the house to be finished and the baby to come out. I hesitate to say that because, as much as she wanted to finally meet this little miracle baby face-to-face, she also remained present enough to truly enjoy every moment, every flutter, every kick, and even every discomfort of this last pregnancy. We had prayed for this, God had delivered, and she didn't want to miss any of it.

By the time the house was completed, we had been living in the RV for more than thirteen months. Central air and heat, a full-size refrigerator, a working sink in the kitchen, more than one bathroom, a cement driveway instead of dirt, a closet that didn't double as a shower, a couch with no scorpions sleeping in the cushions—we were excited about all of it.

That's probably why I was so surprised at how sad we were to say goodbye to the RV. The whole family stood out on the county road as the men drove it away. Our warmth, our security, our refuge, our home for over a year got smaller and smaller as it slowly disappeared over the horizon. There wasn't a dry eye on that hot blacktop as we stood and waved goodbye to an old friend.

Even though my touring still hadn't resumed to any level of

normalcy, the next month flew by. We slowly moved our furniture from the barn and settled into the house, with Amber being careful not to lift anything too heavy. It was a blessing not to be traveling but instead to focus on moving and preparing for the baby's arrival. We had designed the house with four bedrooms—the master, one each for London and Lincoln, and then one extra either for Maverick or to be used as a guest room, depending on God's plan for our family. Lincoln picked the one with the shared bathroom with his little brother.

Only a few weeks from the due date, something crazy and yet not totally unexpected happened. For the first time, our household was stricken with COVID. The kids got it first. It was like a weak cold that they recovered from in a couple of days. But Amber, that was a different story.

She got really, really sick.

She couldn't breathe, couldn't stop coughing, and couldn't get out of bed. Thankfully, I never got sick and did my best at playing nurse. The doctor reassured Amber that the baby would be fine, but her confidence waned with every deep cough, feeling as though she was literally dislodging the baby. Then, each time we felt like she had turned a corner, the lousy fatigue forced her back to bed.

Her symptoms lingered for seventeen days leading up to go time. On August 20, 2021, we rolled into the hospital at 7:00 a.m. They masked her up and took her into pre-op for the cesarean surgery.

I was so nervous.

People say this is supposed to be the best day of a father's life, but to me it's more like one of the worst. My wife is being sliced into, her insides rummaged about, and then there's a rush to yank the baby out between her organs in hopes that he quickly takes his first breath. This was my fourth time to stand next to the doctors and watch this traumatic event, and each time all I could do was sit on a little stool and pray. It was totally out of my hands. But I knew now from life experience that my hands are utterly worthless unless interlocked with my Creator's.

And He delivered.

THE DANCE

Before the surgery the doctors asked us what kind of music we would like to have playing during the delivery.

"Whatever keeps your hands steady," I replied.

They decided to play country music, and that was all right by me. Amber and I both couldn't help but notice the song that randomly played when they first located Maverick.

"Looking back on the memory of the dance we shared beneath the stars above."

It was Garth Brooks's "The Dance."

The doctors reached for the tiny body and wrapped their hands around him as the song continued: "And now I'm glad I didn't know the way it all would end, the way it all would go. Our lives are better left to chance. I could've missed the pain, but I'd have had to miss . . . the dance."[8]

My heart swelled, and my eyes burst with tears when I saw his little face for the first time. I could've missed the pain, but I would have had to miss our gift, our answered prayer, our Maverick.

12

THE LIVING WATER

"Whoever believes in me, as the Scripture has said,
'Out of his heart will flow rivers of living water.'"
John 7:38

RED, PURPLE, BLUE, ORANGE, AND gold streaked across a canvas sky like a marvelous painting as the creaky chains of the porch swing gently rocked back and forth. London and Lincoln giggled and danced barefoot on the green lawn as Amber sat cross-legged on the steps. As I kept up the rhythm of the sway with my foot, baby Mav slept nuzzled in the bend of my elbow.

Soak in this moment because it won't last forever.

I've thought that several times in my life, and it was always right, but I had never fully understood what it meant until now. Nothing lasts forever, but that's exactly what makes life so beautiful, so meaningful. In fact, nothing matters at all until we finally realize that all things are temporary on this earth. When we understand that, we see these things for exactly what they are—small glimpses of the greatest gift: an eternal dwelling in the presence of the river's Source. If His gifts are so good, and it hurts so much to miss them, what would it be like to meet the *Giver* of these gifts? I can't even imagine.

LOSS IS A NECESSARY PART OF LIFE

Consider this. If we never lost any of the gifts of life, how could we really understand how precious they are? How could we possibly know about the brilliance of light if there were no darkness to contrast it?

This is a perspective that I've had to learn.

It's also the contrast presented by the age-old question, How could a good God allow terrible things to happen?

Look, I get it.

Many things in this world seem unfair, or depressing, or demoralizing, or disturbing, or just plain tragic. By design, we live in a world that desperately needs someone to come rescue it. And someone did—Jesus!

When we dive into the Bible, we see a purposefully strong connection between joy and suffering. We're going to have problems on this earth. In fact, we're told it's not just a possibility, it's a given.

Take John 16:33, for instance, where Jesus said, "I have said these things to you, that in me you may have peace. In the world you will have tribulation." Jesus continued with a resolution for us: "But take heart; I have overcome the world."

Read that last part again. That's an incredible promise!

When we are finally redeemed from this broken world and join the ranks in heaven, we will spend the rest of forever, literal eternity, in awe of God for delivering us from all heartache and pain. Living with struggles today gives us another reason to worship God—the One who came to take away the sting of those struggles—because we know they are not the final word. And when we do look to Him, we experience joy. That's how we're designed.

LIVING WITH STRUGGLES TODAY GIVES US ANOTHER REASON TO WORSHIP GOD.

The men and women we read about in the Bible actually rejoiced *in* their suffering. Consider Paul, who was beaten and thrown in jail multiple times, or how Mary, the mother of Jesus, responded when she realized she was pregnant—something that would disgrace her in her society. Neither one considered themselves worthy for the task but faced it, looking to God, finding that joy doesn't come from one's circumstances but from where one is focused.

So I ask, is it really too hard to believe that difficult times can bring about joy?

Think of your favorite movie.

Now remove the antagonist.

Is it still a good movie? No.

If there were no evil, how would we ever see what is good? It would just be—empty.

I can make an example with my favorite sport.

Do you wonder why football players cry tears of joy when they hold up a Super Bowl trophy? It's because they remember how difficult it was to win and know how temporary it is to possess. Those players endured a challenging season. Maybe there was a terrible loss in game two. Or someone had a season-ending injury in game five. Possibly a locker-room dispute in game six. In game eight they might have fought from behind and barely won in overtime. And game ten was lost to a team that they were supposed to beat. I could come up with many examples, but the bottom line is that if a season or football career were perfect with zero adversity and loss, then the trophy ceremony wouldn't be as sweet. The tears of joy come through the pain of suffering.

Loss is not only a part of our lives, it's also necessary for us to truly understand joy. Trusting that God has a plan for His people allows us to not be surprised when the fiery trial comes but instead to rest in the joy that coexists with the suffering. That's my view from the porch today.

The life of Maverick is so mind-blowing to me that it overloads my brain just thinking about it. One life exists because another doesn't. I live in a world now where if I hadn't lost Riv, then I'd lose Mav, but in order to have Mav, I had to lose Riv. A man can go crazy thinking too much about that.

I've often held Maverick up to the large, framed picture of River hanging next to our back door. Riv is sitting on his toy tractor with the 24-volt battery, little hands white-knuckle gripping the steering wheel, and grinning with his sparkling brown eyes. Mav will stare, study it for several seconds, focused on his big brother's face, and then his eyebrows will raise, and he'll crack a wide, toothless, open-mouth smile. What is he thinking about? He has no idea yet, but he will. He will eventually know everything about his brother and what River's brief one thousand days of life meant to his own.

Those are difficult bridges that Amber and I will cross when the time is right and God gives us the words. As far as Maverick is concerned, this is his time, his family; and that's the only way it was ever supposed to be. I can't help but wonder, though, with all of the twists and turns throughout our story, what in the world Maverick's purpose is here. What will his contribution be to this planet during his lifetime? I guess we'll have to wait and see.

LOSS IS A TEACHER

There is such healing in letting go. It breathes new life into every aspect of life. When I let go of River, God gave us Maverick. When I let go of my forever home, God directed my steps to a new, amazing little farm. When I let go of music, it stopped feeling like a job and started to feel like a ministry opportunity. When I let go of the old vision for my family, God opened the door for a new family construct. When I stopped trying to hold on to my own plans for my life, I realized God's plans were far better.

Amber and I are doing our best to live one day at a time, trusting God's leading and prompting as we go. We don't know where the river will lead, but we know that we can trust it, even in the most treacherous parts, because our true forever home is not of this world.

What about you?

Have you ever lost something?

Maybe it was a job. When the thing that provides your income and stability gets taken away, it shakes you to the core.

Maybe it was a dream. Something you wanted your entire life and worked and worked to achieve only to come up short. If you've ever had a moment where you realized your dream isn't going to come to pass, you know how hopeless it can feel. As if the very thing that used to get you out of bed in the morning no longer has the power to do so.

Or perhaps it was a relationship. You met someone, and you thought they were the one. You were convinced you were going to spend the rest of your life with them until they decided they didn't feel the same way. And suddenly, you felt like half of yourself was missing.

Or maybe for you my story hits way too close to home. Because when it comes to loss, your some*thing* is a some*one*.

Whether it was something or someone, we've all experienced loss. It's a part of life. But know this: loss is our teacher. Loss reminds us that nothing here is permanent. When we spend all our time clinging to something, trying to control and preserve it, we miss out on the beauty of what God is doing in our lives. Like navigating a river, we need to let go, surrender, and trust that God's plan for our lives is better than our plan.

I've heard so many people say something like, "I'm embarrassed to tell you that I'm hurting, because you've lost a son, and that loss is much worse than losing my grandpa."

I reject that idea. If you are hurting from the grief of losing a loved one, then you are totally validated in that feeling. Your story is relevant to your life. Pain is pain. It's not something that can be compared. The relationship you had with your grandpa is *real*. I can never relate to that because I didn't live it and I didn't love him; you did.

The place where our stories overlap is in the fact that, once again, our lives are like a river. We can't control the speed or the direction or the obstacles along the way; we can control only how much or how little we surrender to the Source of it. The will flows. God's purpose will stand. How quickly we are able to move forward with the ever-flowing current depends on when we decide to stop resisting it.

GOD IS THE SOURCE OF THE RIVER

The idea of God being the Source of the river is not a new concept. Look how the Bible uses that same comparison:

- "On that day living waters shall flow out from Jerusalem, half of them to the eastern sea and half of them to the western sea. It shall continue in summer as in winter." (Zechariah 14:8)
- "The water was flowing down from below the south end of the threshold of the temple, south of the altar." (Ezekiel 47:1)
- "Then the angel showed me the river of the water of life, bright as crystal, flowing from the throne of God and of the Lamb." (Revelation 22:1)
- "There is a river whose streams make glad the city of God, the holy habitation of the Most High. God is in the midst of

her; she shall not be moved; God will help her when morning dawns." (Psalm 46:4–5)
- "The earth was without form and void, and darkness was over the face of the deep. And the Spirit of God was hovering over the face of the waters." (Genesis 1:2)

And what the Bible says about surrendering to the Source:

- "When you pass through the waters, I will be with you; and through the rivers, they shall not overwhelm you; when you walk through fire you shall not be burned, and the flame shall not consume you." (Isaiah 43:2)
- "Whoever believes in me, as the Scripture has said, 'Out of his heart will flow rivers of living water.'" (John 7:38)
- "Whoever drinks of the water that I will give him will never be thirsty again. The water that I will give him will become in him a spring of water welling up to eternal life." (John 4:14)
- "For whoever would save his life will lose it, but whoever loses his life for my sake will find it." (Matthew 16:25)

A NEW WAY OF RIVER RAFTING

If you learn anything from this book, let it be this: ditch your oars and burn the boat. No matter how much mental strength and endurance you think you have, when you meet the waterfall that eventually comes to us all, oars and a boat won't help you. The only thing you'll be able to trust is God and His Word, the Bible.

With that, here are three practices that I've developed to help me navigate the river.

1. Read the Bible Every Day

The Bible isn't a game of telephone where Scripture has been lost or corrupted after so many translations. These days we have access to the ancient Hebrew and Greek texts, and we have the technology to translate directly from our own phone if we so choose.

We can trust it.

And get this: the one and only true God revealed in those Scriptures is *totally* in control. There's an old Sunday school song titled "He's Got the Whole World in His Hands." Yes, He has a plan, He has a purpose, and it's always good. I no longer question that when things get tough. In fact, instead of crying out, "Why, God?" I've changed the question to, "What, God? What are You trying to show me through this trial?" I haven't always received clear answers, but every time I've asked this, while praising Him for the perfect plan that I simply can't yet see, I've felt a peace about it.

Think of it this way. Our conversation with God goes in two directions. We pray—that's us talking. And we read the Bible—that's God talking back to us. The scriptures that we gather give us everything we need to understand life's winding river. Most books we read to understand something, but the more we read the Bible, the more we realize that it understands us.

I don't substitute anything for my time reading the Bible. My schedule keeps me pretty busy, but nothing takes me away from my daily reading. I do this as if my life depends on it. Before I begin reading, I close my eyes and pray, *God, open my eyes to the truth that I need to see today. Reveal to me Your wisdom, and open my heart to understand it.*

I don't trade that time for anything else. Devotionals are great, but they are never a replacement for the full context of what I might need to hear. Scripture is life-changing, something

I need daily to refuel and equip me for dealing with life's battles. In fact, each morning I wake up thinking, *I can't wait to see how God will speak to me today!*

2. Surrender to the Source

I steer clear of traditional meditation because it teaches us to surrender our thoughts by clearing our minds. I don't want empty thoughts and open space that could become an invitation to the Enemy. I will never underestimate his power again after my darkest night. Instead, I fill my mind with God's Word as revealed in the Bible. In 2 Corinthians 10:5 Paul said, "Take every thought captive to obey Christ."

Whether we realize it or not, there is a war, a spiritual battle raging all around us. I will never again be ambushed while holding useless wooden weapons.

Check this out. The apostle Paul put it this way in Ephesians 6:11–13: "Put on the whole armor of God, that you may be able to stand against the schemes of the devil. For we do not wrestle against flesh and blood, but against the rulers, against the authorities, against the cosmic powers over this present darkness, against the spiritual forces of evil in the heavenly places. Therefore take up the whole armor of God, that you may be able to withstand in the evil day." Whoa! That's pretty black-and-white!

I also tread very cautiously with any kind of self-help material. *The Miracle Morning* book taught me a valuable technique in scheduling my mornings before I begin tackling the day, and I'm grateful for that. The majority of that time now is dedicated to reading the Bible. I read four chapters each morning from a reading plan called the M'Cheyne Reading Plan,[9] and I never skip it—even if I'm on an early flight. I read slowly, research parts that I don't understand, take notes, highlight, and then post a piece of Scripture that spoke to me that day on social media with a one-line commentary. That helps me stay accountable. *The Miracle Morning* helped me build this routine.

I still exercise, journal, read books, listen to podcasts and sermons, and eat healthy, but none of this rules my life. I don't surrender to or put faith in any of it, especially through severe suffering. (I can guarantee that losing my son River won't be the last severe suffering in my life.)

Generally, self-help teaches that the problem is outside us and the solution comes from within. The Bible teaches that the problem comes from within and the solution is outside us. There are places in the river where no amount of paddling can keep your boat upright. That's why I surrender to the Source and not to my own ability. If you're like me and you've been sucked into the self-help religion, hear my warning—it cultivates pride, suppresses humility, and won't save you when you need it the most.

3. Hang with Like-Minded People

Lastly, I surround myself with other like-minded believers. Small groups, worship, and church services are not a chore to me anymore; they are a lifeline. It's a higher priority than sleep or food or the Dallas Cowboys. If I'm working out of town, I'll find a local congregation. I've met many new lifetime friends this way. If the kids don't want to go, we drag them out anyway, even if we have to miss baseball games or other events. I want them to know where Mom and Dad's priorities stack up. The church is described as the bride of Christ. Would I ever tell a friend that I love him but don't like his wife? I don't think we would be friends anymore after that.

I'm a sinner. I've made mistakes in the past, and I will continue to make mistakes in the future, so I walk into church with that kind of humility. I praise God in His house for saving an undeserving rebel like me. Like the hymn says, "Amazing grace, how sweet the sound that saved a wretch like me."

THE NAPKIN

John Newton, the hymn writer of "Amazing Grace," was a slave boat captain in the 1700s when he was saved not from a drunken ambush in Boise, Idaho, like me, but from a literal violent storm in the North Atlantic Ocean. Similar to me, it took several months until he totally surrendered and was reborn. Immediately after his rebirth, he was passionate about spending time with as many church leaders as possible.[10] I felt that too.

In early 2020, I filled my calendar not with tour dates but with lunch meetings with different pastors around the Austin area. I wanted to know everything about God that they could tell me. I asked questions like:

What is your faith story?
What does your Bible study routine look like?
What are your thoughts on this or that biblical doctrine?
How do you pray?

One day, a pastor friend asked me to speak at a men's breakfast conference at the church we attended weekly. The topic was on suffering. I had serious doubts about my qualifications for an event like this, but my friend reassured me that God doesn't call the qualified, He qualifies the called.

The date was June 11, 2020. My mind raced as I scrambled to piece together enough thoughts for a twenty-five-minute talk, but I didn't even think about the date.

June 11.

It was exactly one year to the day from when I had walked into that same church for the first time for Riv's funeral. Was it a coincidence or a glitch in the Matrix? I knew better than that. God was speaking. He was restoring. No suffering is wasted. There is purpose on the other side of surrender.

I'm not sure if any of those men benefited from what I said that day, but I did. I learned that by sharing my story of pain and redemption, God was answering my question.

Not the one that asked God why.

The one that asked God, *What are You trying to show me through this heartache?*

God responded through His Word, "Fear not, for I am with you; be not dismayed, for I am your God; I will strengthen you, I will help you, I will uphold you with my righteous right hand" (Isaiah 41:10).

God was reminding me to depend on Him. He would be there to pick me up and push me forward from the bottom of the river's waterfall.

A few months later, after a concert in Indiana, I was invited to again speak at a church the following Sunday morning. The date wasn't significant this time, but the name of the church sure was. I stood in the parking lot with the lead pastor, smiling as we gazed up at the building. In huge letters on the side of the church it read, Granger Community Church. I had to laugh at the irony. Through my stubbornness and my continued doubts about the call to preach, God literally had to write my name on the side of the building to confirm it.

I wrote a sermon and was responsibly prepared to deliver it, but I just didn't know how to end the message. Navigating my own grief was hard enough, but now I wasn't sure that I was ready to shepherd other people's pain.

That's when I found it.

There was a folded-up napkin stuffed into my pocket in the blue jeans I had worn at the concert the night before. I don't remember anyone putting it there, but it must have been from a fan at the meet and greet. I unfolded it and read the words as tears filled my eyes. In scribbled writing, someone wrote, "After you have suffered a little while, the God of all grace, who has called you to his eternal glory in Christ, will himself restore, confirm, strengthen, and establish you" (1 Peter 5:10).

I didn't question it anymore. That's how I would end the sermon that morning. I was moving downstream with no boat and no oars.

MY TRUE FOREVER HOME

There's a little, white, nineteenth-century church tucked away down a forgotten backroad in the Hill Country. Next to it in a field of wildflowers and native bluestem, scorched by a relentless Texas sun, is a cemetery. The grass has grown over River's grave now, hiding the once fresh red dirt that the excavator turned over.

I'm here now.

The sky is blue and wide with plenty of room for the midday sun to make its journey all the way down beneath the rolling horizon of cedar and oak trees. There are no rainbows today.

I like coming here. I walk the grounds and listen to the wind whip over the top of the old headstones. There are so many of them—so many names, so many dates and dashes. I once stood out here with my family mourning the loss of our baby boy, just as those families had stood and mourned their loss.

All of them.

I find comfort in that. Many fathers stood here over the newly dug grave of their child, or wife, or parent, or friend. And then within a span of a few decades, they, too, joined them in the earth. Life in this world is a vapor, so fleeting and so short. This old cemetery puts that in perspective for me. My little plot of dirt is here too, waiting for me, right next to River.

My bones will waste away in this ground. But just like our house with the fruit trees and honeybees, it's not my forever home either. My true forever home is a place where all tears will be wiped away, with no more suffering and no more pain. That's the place I choose to focus on—the river's final destination.

Like a river, life is full of twists and turns.

Like a river, I will encounter storms, debris, shallows, deep, calm, and turbulence.

But like a river, regardless of the obstacles, I will never fail to find my path downstream. I'll trust the Source to carry me home. And when I finally arrive, I'll be met by a little barefoot, redheaded boy who can run like a river. What a glorious day that will be!

AFTERWORD

IN 2020 AROUND THE ONE-YEAR anniversary of River going to heaven, I was seeing the word *river* everywhere. This is a common psychological effect called Baader Meinhof that happens when something significant is on your mind and you notice it throughout your daily life. For example, when a woman gets engaged, she all of a sudden can't help but notice white dresses and wedding venues advertised on billboards that she hadn't noticed before.

The word *river* is unavoidable. It's on maps and street signs and shopping centers all over the world. This was a matter of torment for me. On one particular day when the Baader Meinhof effect was having its way with me, within a span of just a few minutes I saw *river* four different times while driving in my hometown. Clutching the steering wheel and making a right turn onto I-35, I saw the word for a fifth time. This was too much. I glared through the windshield into the blue sky and shouted, "What?! What are you trying to show me, God?" In that moment as I was merging onto the interstate, a big eighteen-wheeler roared past me. In giant blue letters on the trailer was the unmistakable word: *Peace*. Next to the word was the silhouette of a large blue dove. The message was received loud and clear.

A few months later, Amber and I were driving back in silence after learning that she was miscarrying the first embryo. Once again the same truck passed us in yet another thundering confirmation moment.

Look, I'm not implying that God is in the business of sending miracle tractor trailers to me down Texas interstates (even though He certainly could). He speaks His truth through His ever-living Word, the Bible, and when we're familiar with that Word, we can know beyond a shadow of a doubt that God *does* desire peace for those who love Him. That's a promise from Jesus. My hope is that this book can be a beacon of light to you, as those giant blue letters were to me.

One of my favorite hymns, *It Is Well With My Soul*, says:

> When peace, like a river, attendeth my way,
> When sorrows like sea billows roll;
> Whatever my lot, Thou hast taught me to say,
> It is well, it is well with my soul.

Today, three and a half years after River went to Jesus, those lyrics ring true for me. It is well with my soul. There are occasional, fleeting moments of sadness and hopeful grief, but we have healed well, thanks to God. There are no remnants of depression because my God-gifted joy is just too abundant. If you picked up this book in desperation for relief in your loss, look at this eighteen-wheeler peace trailer I'm showing you. My journey can be yours. I'm not special. I'm not unique. I'm certainly not deserving of grace, and there are only two words that can complete that thought—*But God*.

I've been praying for you, the reader, continually since before I even penned the first sentence of this manuscript. I have prayed for your eyes and ears to be opened to the gospel in a fresh way. I have prayed for your restoration and your healing. I have praised

God for the hearts he has prepared to receive this message, and for the family or friends or pastor who gifted you this book, and even for the divine encounter you had with it when it first caught your attention to pick it up.

My greatest desire is for this book to mirror what that YouTube sermon did for me in my pickup truck on that county road on March 1, 2020. I say this because Romans 10:17 says, "So faith comes from hearing, and hearing comes through the word of Christ." Recently the pastor from that YouTube video, John Piper, received news about me and my story. A mutual friend, Mark Dever, encouraged me to send him a short video message explaining what had happened on that day, because (according to Mark) Pastor John doesn't think he's a good evangelist. *Seriously?* Despite my reluctant insecurities, I sent a video message, and Pastor John graciously replied with this:

> Dear Granger,
>
> Thank you for the moving and beautiful and encouraging video testimony that you sent through Mark Dever. As I ponder the grace of God at that moment in your life, I circle back to Romans 5:5. "God's love has been poured into our hearts through the Holy Spirit who has been given to us." What else can we say, but that he has done it, and it is marvelous in our eyes? Glad with you on this Lord's Day morning.
>
> —John Piper

He has done it. Oh how I long to be able to echo that back to you, my friend reading my story. As I sit finishing the last few words of this book, it's been almost a year since I began writing. Even in that short period of time, things have continued to change in my life.

Little Maverick is walking now. How surreal is the thought

that soon he'll be the same age as his older brother River? The hands of time are certainly not slowing down. It's upon this realization that I'm surrendering to some life-altering changes in my career.

Although my music fans don't know this yet, I've made the decision to follow the unrelenting call from God upon my life and end my touring career. To put it plainly, there's just not time for it anymore. There are too many hurting people, too many lost people, and too many people without a Savior in Jesus. John 3:36 says, "Whoever believes in the Son has eternal life; whoever does not obey the Son shall not see life, but the wrath of God remains on him." The reality of that burden is too great, and the stakes are too high for me to continue in a remotely obscure distance from the front lines of the battle.

I love music touring, and that's what makes the sacrifice significant for me. It's been a wildly focused passion of mine for twenty-four years, but God has reduced that passion for music touring and raised it proportionately for missionary touring. This passion literally kept me up at night until I finally submitted to it. I will still travel, only with a very different purpose. I'll continue preaching at churches, and I am pursuing a master's degree at Southern Baptist Theological Seminary. Other than that, my future is none of my business. What a freeing feeling that is.

I know people will think that I've completely lost my mind to abandon a fruitful career, but I assure you that I've actually finally found it. Close friends of mine have asked, "How will you pay the bills?" It's true that touring has been my main source of income for nearly half of my life. But I would ask this: After everything God has fulfilled in my life since I've surrendered to his plan, would I dare question his sufficiency now? Absolutely not. Let this book be evidence of his providence in my life.

In the book of Joshua, God led his people to the banks of

the Jordan River. At last after forty years of wandering in the wilderness, the people of Israel stood only a stone's throw from the promised land. There was one final obstacle in their journey: a brimming, turbulent, harvest-season river. God told Joshua to command the priests carrying the ark of the covenant to step into the raging waters and, once their feet were still and firm upon the rock on the river bottom, God would *then* stop the water and enable them to cross safely on dry ground.

I, too, have wandered for forty years in the wilderness. Here I am at the banks of the roaring river. The promised land is close. In faith I will step into the water, and my feet will rest firmly upon the rock. The next chapter of my life has only just begun!

YOU REALLY, REALLY NEED TO READ THIS . . .

ARE YOU HURTING? ARE YOU stuck? Are you lost? I can relate. Jesus says in John 5:6, "Do you want to be healed?" I have good news for you, and I'm really glad you've made it to the end of this book. It doesn't matter where you grew up or how much money you make or what color skin you have or what you used to believe or how badly you've messed things up. Jesus says, "Come to me all, you who are weary and burdened, and I will give you rest" (Matthew 11:28 NIV).

I can hear your question already, "But *how* do I come to Him?" Maybe you're a Dog-Tag Christian like I was, and you're confused as to why you don't feel saved or why you see no difference in your life than a nonbeliever. Maybe at some point in your life you repeated the Sinner's Prayer and asked Jesus into your heart. There's one problem with that: repeating the Sinner's Prayer isn't biblical. It creates a false sense of salvation. What if you committed murder and I marched you over to the victim's mother and asked you to repeat a prayer of repentance to gain her forgiveness? That would be ridiculous.

Do you remember what I mentioned back in chapter 8? In John 6:44, Jesus says, "No one can come to me unless the Father who sent me draws him." I want to stop here and give you a vote of confidence. If you're still reading, it certainly seems as though you *are* being drawn. Others would have put this book down by now. You'll notice this by a growing desire to know more and by a compounding realization that you are *loved*. What I desperately want you to see from my story is this: our own effort in earning our way to God is futile. The Bible says that our good works are dirty rags to Him. Ephesians 2:8–9 says, "For by grace you have been saved through faith. And this is not your own doing; it is the gift of God, not a result of works, so that no one may boast." Romans 11:5–6 says, "So too at the present time there is a remnant, chosen by grace. But if it is by grace, it is no longer on the basis of works; otherwise, grace would no longer be grace." After my rebirth on that county road, I absolutely devoured Bible reading. My soul shouted at me, *I'm part of that remnant! I am loved! I am yours, Jesus! Have mercy on me, a sinner!* It was like finding gold in a mountain, and I just couldn't stop digging! For years I tried so hard on my river to use my oars to paddle to shore. Nothing changed for me until I surrendered them, and even that surrender was by the grace of God.

So then you might ask, What happened to you in chapter 8? I felt the draw, I heard the gospel preached, and God made me a new creation. Romans 1:16 says, "[The gospel] is the power of God for salvation." The apostle Paul later said in Romans 10:17, "So faith comes from hearing, and hearing through the word of Christ." The seeds were planted somewhere along my journey, and in God's timing, the plant was grown.

Here's my point: Are you drowning in your own river? Let me tell you the gospel. *Hear* it. It in itself contains the power of God to save your life like it did mine. Here it is:

We are all sinners in need of a savior because we all fall short of God's glory. God came to earth in the person of Jesus to redeem and gather His people. He healed the sick, cast out demons, taught about the kingdom of heaven, and fulfilled God's law perfectly like no one ever could. He was crucified on a cross and became a substitute for our sins, paying in full the debt we could not afford to pay. Three days later He rose from the dead, confirming His divinity in front of hundreds of eyewitnesses. He said that anyone who believes that He is Lord and turns from their sin will have peace, rest, and most importantly, eternal life in the presence of God. Anyone who does not trust in Him alone will not.

My heartfelt prayer in writing this book is that this simple yet profound gospel message will invade your heart in a radical way. Trust me, you'll know when it does.

INFANT SWIM RESCUE GUIDE

THIS BOOK WOULD NOT BE complete without having a conversation about water safety. If even one life can be spared, then it's worth it for River's legacy. I am confident that this information can save lives.

No one should be exempt from reading this section. Whether or not you or someone in your neighborhood has a pool, whether or not you have children or grandchildren, know neighbors with children, take vacations around water with children, or simply live on planet earth with children, we all need to know more than just the basics of water safety.

Drowning is usually silent, and it can occur in only a matter of seconds.[11] Disregard every movie you've seen with someone splashing around in a panic. Children reflexively inhale water directly into their lungs and lose consciousness.[12]

These facts are not typically discussed by pediatricians despite the fact that drowning is the number one cause of death for children under the age of four and number two in ages one through fourteen.[13] Sixty-nine percent of drowning deaths of children under the age of five happened when they were not expected to be swimming.[14] Bathtubs, toilets, buckets, ponds, pools, oceans, streams, rivers, and lakes are all drowning risks. The guidelines for water safety are multilayered, meaning a reliance on only one or two safety measures is not enough. Simply thinking that child supervision is sufficient is deadly. Simply relying on a pool fence is just as deadly—you can take it from me.

Before I get into the layers of protection, let's first establish some general rules. Regardless of what the culture teaches, we need to stop making water fun before our children have the skills to survive in it. A nice fire in the fireplace is wonderful on a cold winter day, but we would never allow a three-year-old to get too close to the flames before they understand the danger. Here's the rule: if your child does not have the skills to survive in the water, then you need to hold them at all times. Avoid the temptation of allowing them to jump off the side into your arms, thereby giving them a false sense of their own abilities.

Here are multilayered measures of protection to consider:

- Supervision is the first and most critical line of defense. Always designate a "Water Guardian," and change the guard every fifteen minutes.
- Pools should have a permanent four-sided fence around them. Do not allow a child to play and/or climb on the fence. Remove patio furniture that may be pushed or pulled and used as a ladder.
- Always use Coast Guard–approved life jackets in lakes, rivers, or the ocean.
- Do not rely on floatation devices during swim time, especially "floaties," which put the child in a drowning position and provide false security.
- If a child is missing, look for them in the water first.
- Buy swim clothes with bright colors.
- Aim jets and in-floor jets to the shallow end of the pool.

- Waterfalls in pool areas create a noise level that may compete with a cry for help.
- Never answer your phone or go get a towel during supervision.
- Carry a cell phone with you at all times to call 911 in an emergency.
- Outdoor toys should be stored in an area that is isolated from the pool deck. Never store toys in the pool.
- Install door and pool alarms. Make sure all doors leading outside are locked and armed, including doggie doors.
- Always keep the cover on a spa.
- Never leave your child alone in the bathtub, even when getting a towel.
- Never leave your child under the care of another child.
- Never allow a child to ride in the front of a boat.
- Learn CPR and update skills regularly.
- Enroll young children in ISR's (Infant Swim Resource) Self-Rescue Lessons (including refresher sessions) from the age of six months up to six years.

When Maverick turned eight months old, we enrolled him in ISR. Because of our history, this was a heart-wrenching yet empowering experience. In just a few weeks, Mav was able to tumble off the edge of a pool deck headfirst into the water, rotate his body, float on his back, and find the air.

Check out these links for more information:

WATER SAFETY

- National Drowning Prevention Alliance (www.ndpa.org)
- CAST Water Safety Foundation (www.castwatersafety.org/printables-library)

- Sea Star's "Important Keys to Water Safety" (www.seastarisr.com/water-safety)
- Levi's Legacy (www.levislegacy.com)
- The LV Project (www.thelvproject.org)
- The Sylas Project's "Water Safety Tips & Checklist" (www.thesylasproject.org/water-safety)
- Self-rescue tips from CAST (www.castwatersafety.org/what-is-self-rescue)

SURVIVAL SWIM

- Infant Swimming Resources (www.infantswim.com)
- Infant Aquatics (www.infantaquatics.com)

PERSONAL REFLECTION AND GROUP DISCUSSION GUIDE

1. Granger uses the metaphor of a rushing river to express the nature of life. How is your life like a river? How do you navigate it?
2. What coping mechanisms do you use to get through hard times? How effective are they when you come to new challenges or unexpected twists?
3. What life-changing losses have you experienced? What losses and griefs have you known that others might label as less significant? How do you grieve all of these things in similar ways?
4. What aspects of your life have you felt the need to control? Imagine surrendering those areas to God. What would that look like practically?
5. What are the limits of your own ability to help yourself out of dark experiences? What role does God play in these times?
6. What makes surrender difficult? What beliefs or fears stand in your way?
7. How do you see that God is using your suffering for a purpose? What do you believe about that notion?

8. What does it mean to you to have integrity through the darkest seasons of your life?
9. Granger says that grief and joy—not happiness, but a deep inner peace—can coexist. If you have ever experienced this, what made that happen for you? How would you describe it to someone who hasn't experienced it?
10. Jesus said, "If anyone loves me, he will keep my word." Granger realized after hearing this that he had never fully read the Bible. He soon experienced significant healing when he began reading the Bible daily. What would this kind of routine look like in your life?
11. Granger writes: "If you learn anything from this book, let it be this: ditch your oars and burn the boat. No matter how much mental strength and endurance you think you have, when you meet the waterfall that eventually comes to us all, oars and a boat won't help you. The only thing you'll be able to trust is God and His Word, the Bible." What might it mean for you to ditch your "oars" and burn your "boat"?

NOTES

1. Granger Smith (@grangersmith), Instagram photo, August 23, 2019, https://www.instagram.com/p/B1h_zcgpE70/?igshid=MDJmNzVkMjY%3D.
2. This poem is frequently misattributed to Ralph Waldo Emerson but comes from an essay written by Bessie A. Stanley of Lincoln, Kansas, in 1905. See "He Has Achieved Success Who Has Lived Well, Laughed Often and Loved Much," Quote Investigator, June 26, 2012, https://quoteinvestigator.com/2012/06/26/define-success.
3. Drew Weisholtz, "Granger Smith's Wife Responds to 'Cruel' Comments About Son Who Died," Today, August 25, 2021, https://www.today.com/parents/granger-smiths-wife-responds-cruel-comments-son-died-rcna1767.
4. "Popular Verses: A Video Devotional with John Piper—Day 5," YouVersion, https://www.bible.com/reading-plans/608-popular-verses-video-devo-piper/day/5.
5. Desiring God, "How to Seek the Holy Spirit," YouTube, February 2, 2018, https://www.youtube.com/watch?v=xqgeT26BAnE.
6. Rachel Gurevich, "The Chances for IVF Pregnancy Success," Verywell Family, October 26, 2022, https://www.verywellfamily.com/what-are-the-chances-for-ivf-success-1960213.
7. Dr. R. Bruce Winders, "Texas Legend," *The Alamo*, accessed February 8, 2023, https://www.thealamo.org/remember/military-occupation/samuel-a-maverick.

8. Garth Brooks. "The Dance." Track 10 on *Garth Brooks*. Capitol Records, 1989, CD.
9. "M'Cheyne Bible Reading Plan," BibleGateway, https://www.biblegateway.com/reading-plans/mcheyne/next?version=NIV; and "M'Cheyne One Year Reading Plan," YouVersion, https://www.bible.com/reading-plans/24-mcheyne-one-year-reading-plan.
10. "John Newton: Reformed slave trader," *Christianity Today*, accessed February 8, 2023, https://www.christianitytoday.com/history/people/pastorsandpreachers/john-newton.html.
11. Brianna McCabe, "8 Truths About Drowning and 'Dry Drowning' Revealed," Hackensack Meridian Health, July 9, 2019, https://www.hackensackmeridianhealth.org/en/HealthU/2019/07/09/8-truths-about-drowning-and-dry-drowning-revealed#.Y5JgRi2cbOQ.
12. "What a drowning prevention specialist wants parents to know," Children's Health, https://www.childrens.com/health-wellness/facts-about-childhood-drowning.
13. "Drowning Facts," Centers for Disease Control and Prevention, https://www.cdc.gov/drowning/facts/index.html.
14. "Water Safety and Drowning Prevention," Child Safety Center, https://www.childsafety.center/water-safety.html.

ACKNOWLEDGMENTS

AS WITH ANYTHING I'VE EVER done with my platform, my name might be on the cover, but it's because of the teamwork behind the scenes that this book made it into your hands. I'm indebted to so many along my journey.

My brother and manager, Tyler Smith, you were the first call I made when I felt the urge to write a book. Like you have always done with me, you gave me wise counsel, pointed me down a solid path, and managed my expectations. However, now that the book is out, your real work is only beginning! I can't begin to imagine a better advocate for spreading such a delicate family story than you.

Kyle Olund, thank you for your friendship, your talent as an editor, and your flexibility with someone as stubborn as me. I'm sorry that this book isn't as good as the masterpiece you edited, *Wild at Heart*.

Esther Fedorkevich, is there a better literary agent in the world? Um, no. You have embraced my story and my vision and granted me priority from day one. Thank you!

Ryan Wekenman, you were the WD-40 that opened this rusty hinge. I cherish our original coffee chats, discussing what direction and purpose this book would take. I needed someone to push me off my comfortable edge, and you did that with such pastoral grace.

Mom, I love you. I'm sorry Dad got an entire chapter written about him and you didn't. But you cooked me brisket, beans, and corn bread while I wrote, and that's probably more valuable anyway.

My brother Parker, I'm only putting you in the acknowledgments because Tyler felt bad that he was included and you weren't. Just kidding. Your calm, collected, unbiased nudges have carried so much weight with me over the years. I'm so excited to see what God has in store for your life!

Amber, this book could not have been completed without you. In fact, without you as a witness, I'm not sure anyone would even believe half of it. Next to His saving grace, you are the single greatest gift God has ever given me. I can't wait to read your book one day. People need to hear your side of the story as well!

London, Lincoln, and Maverick, how old will you be when you finally read this book? Will the memory of River still be bright, or will it be faint and dim? I pray that God will give me the strength to answer your questions with Spirit-filled boldness when the time comes and you come asking. I can tell you right now without wavering that God orchestrated a masterpiece in our family. When we surrender our trust to Jesus, we no longer need to explain the unexplainable. We no longer need to ask the question, *Why?* Instead, we simply ask, *What will you have for me to do now, Lord?*

ABOUT THE AUTHOR

Granger Smith is an award-winning, platinum-selling, American country music singer-songwriter who fell in love with music at an early age. Over the course of his groundbreaking career, Granger has amassed a massive and rabid audience known as Yee Yee Nation, built through heavy touring and grassroots fan engagement. He has released ten studio albums, one live album, and two EPs. Granger has charted over eight singles on the Billboard country charts, including the number one hit "Backroad Song." He is a highly sought-after speaker, actor, author, and host of the nationally syndicated iHeartRadio show *After Midnite with Granger Smith*. In 2017 he started the *Granger Smith Podcast*, where he discusses matters of faith, family, music, and the outdoors, while spreading messages of integrity, honor, truth, and restoration grounded in a Christian worldview. Granger's social media following exceeds twelve million, with more than one billion online video views. Granger and his wife, Amber, live north of Austin, Texas, with their kids London, Lincoln, and Maverick.

From the Publisher

GREAT BOOKS

ARE EVEN BETTER WHEN THEY'RE SHARED!

Help other readers find this one:

- Post a review at your favorite online bookseller
- Post a picture on a social media account and share why you enjoyed it
- Send a note to a friend who would also love it—or better yet, give them a copy

Thanks for reading!

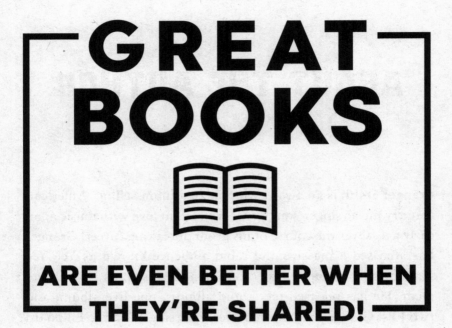